MUSIC EDUCATION

IN ACTION

by

RUSSELL VAN DYKE MORGAN, MUS.D.

and

HAZEL NOHAVEC MORGAN, PH.D., MUS.D.
Lecturer in Music Education
Northwestern University

NEIL A. KJOS MUSIC CO., Publishers
Chicago, Illinois

Preface

This book is designed as a basic text for those preparing to teach in the general elementary grades or as teachers of school music; for those who are actively engaged in music education; and as a source of reference. It is the outcome of many years of teaching experience at all grade levels, of college experience in preparing teachers of school music, and serving as advisers for graduate students majoring in music education.

Because teachers should know specifically the goals to be achieved through the teaching of music, they will need to be aware of the basic principles involved and the practices which will enable them to accomplish these goals.

This volume is intended for those who desire to help boys and girls to have a satisfactory contact with and an understanding of music as they proceed from the kindergarten through the elementary grades, and through junior and senior high school.

In this book will be found music standards set forth according to activities and grade levels, as well as general methods of approach and techniques of procedure presented in the light of present day trends in general education and applied directly to the field of music education.

THE AUTHORS

Contents

Appendix

SOME TRENDS AND NEEDS IN MUSIC EDUCATION

The present world situation coupled with the immediate past has focused attention upon all phases of education with a strength and urgency unprecedented in the annals of world history. Political leaders, top military personnel, economists, the clergy, and even the rank and file of our democratic citizenry are asking for the answer to an all important question.

"What can be set in motion *now* so that all peoples can live satisfactorily and happily in a fashion which will be mutually beneficial?"

Scientific investigation and experience have given us the answer. It is one word and that word is EDUCATION. Education in its broadest sense means to give information and abilities which will result in satisfaction within the individual, and further to instill ideals which will result in satisfactory living with our fellow-men. This can be done, and the consequences if this is not done should be fully realized.

Before any program can be formulated and put into action, music teachers, private as well as school music teachers, must have a crusading conviction that music is a beneficent agent for making life more satisfactory; that it is one of the most important sources of spiritual strength; that it is particularly important in the development of proper attitudes, and is capable of exerting controls and releases for the feelings and emotions. It is the responsibility of the music teacher to direct this power so that it will reach not only into the whole life of our country, but into the future, and to all parts of all countries.

Expansion of Public Education. There is a definite trend over the whole United States to extend education at public expense one year downward to include the four-year-olds (pre-kindergarten), and to extend it upwards to include the thirteenth and fourteenth grades (junior college), as a part of the local educational plan. This is meaningful for music education because enrichments can be begun a year earlier and the blossom which begins to flower in the secondary school can be brought to higher fruition.

Activities and Courses. Some changes are taking place in the type of musical activities as well as in the content of traditional courses. In the lower grades, when speaking of fundamentals of music, most people mention the ability to read music. It is granted that this is an important aspect of music education, however, readiness for note reading has been located scientifically in about the fourth grade or when children are eight to ten years of age. Before children have reached the age where note reading can be taught efficiently, they should sing many, many songs, become sensitized to rhythm and mood, and be surrounded with musical loveliness.

It is granted that every individual who is not pitch deaf or who does not have defective vocal cords can be taught to sing a tune and to get pleasure from the activity. Likewise, every individual can be taught to play some instrument to the extent that he can be an acceptable part of a group. It would follow, therefore, that continued emphasis upon singing and playing should be made from the first grade throughout the entire school life of the child. This will result in better choirs, bands, orchestras, small ensembles, and solo performance. Better, not only in the quality of performance, but better in the cultural, sociological, and psychological outcomes.

There is a trend for the fusion of the social and art values of music, and this must be recognizable in continued musical activities after graduation. Many alumnae choirs and junior civic orchestras are flourishing. This phase should be extended to even the smallest communities where county organizations are possible.

School Music Materials. Recent major series of basic elementary music texts have many innovations in methods of presentation and music content which expedite and enrich the whole elementary school music program. Importance has been placed not only upon singing and playing, but also upon listening, dancing, and composing.

These books contain folk material, standard selections, art songs, and a few songs by contemporary composers. It is regrettable that more present-day composers are not interested in writing music for the elementary level in our schools. This is the one place of all others where children and young people can become acquainted with the modern idiom used by these composers. There is a serious need for present-day composers to realize that there is no other possible area where children can gain an understanding and a desire for the modern idiom, than the elementary grades. The senior high school and college level seems a little too late. When composers make an effort to learn about the abilities of children and the basic philosophy which underlies elementary education, more contemporary music will find a place in basic and supplimentary music text books.

Satisfaction Through Music. There is a definite trend away from the purely mechanical aspects of music toward enriched and related

2

activities. Musicians would do well to remember that music can be a hand-maiden as well as to occupy the center of the stage. It is the responsibility of the music educator to recognize and aid in the musical satisfaction of the rank and file of music consumers. All musicians, and especially those who teach, must aid in reducing the gap between popular entertainment music and that of concert and opera repertoire. If students are given a basis for judgment of musical values, their choice need not be feared and there will be assurance that the good will survive, and further, that it will permeate the music of the world.

Most of a teacher's time is spent trying to keep the slow pupil up with the average one while the gifted child takes care of himself. True equality of opportunity in education, which is assumed as a goal towards which all strive, must mean that no hazard of geography nor parental economic status must be allowed to stand between the gifted child and the development he is capable of achieving. The student of great musical talent who has the misfortune to be born in a community providing no stimulus, or a family unable to recognize or support the training of these unusual gifts, should have some place to turn for financial aid and guidance. More scholarships are urgently needed from both public and private sources.

Liberalized Curriculum. The curriculum in conservatories and music departments of colleges and universities should be liberalized to the extent that through examination, gifted students may accelerate or fulfill pre-requisites in a minimum of time. A few schools have realized that to give all students substantially the same education is not to equalize at all because few students, as individuals at the college level, get exactly what they need most or desire. Something truly beneficial and practical must be done for the gifted child.

Expanded Techniques

Active participation has always been one of the chief objectives of music education. Numerous scientific devices are available which will enhance previous teaching techniques provided they are used properly. The use of audio-visual techniques is becoming universal.

Radio networks have educational directors and programs designed especially for school use. Many large cities have their own FM (frequency modulation) stations and use radio in all phases of education. Administrators, classroom teachers, and children are enthusiastic about well organized instruction in music by radio. Four types of music lessons are now being used successfully, (a) for basic instruction, (b) for supplementary purposes, (c) for promotional purposes, and (d) for recreation. These lessons come from three sources, (a) specially written and produced by the school music staff, (b) specially written and produced by a commercial staff, and (c) sustaining programs. The specific purpose of these lessons are chiefly for, (a) skills and techniques, (b) illustrations to establish concepts of acceptable interpretation and tone quality, (c) appreciation, (d) information, and (e) leisure.

Television channels have been allocated for educational purposes and investigation of methods and techniques need to be continued in order to utilize all the facets of music teaching possible by its use. It has been proved that information received simultaneously by ear and eye tends to be retained.

An era of rapid expansion of film teaching aids, both vocal and instrumental, lies immediately ahead. Professional musicians and music educators should give attention to directing this expansion and to the proper utilization of this medium.

The wire and tape recorders, the mirrorphone, the strobescope, the audio-frequency oscillator, phonoscope, sound level meter and sound analyzer, the audiometer, the oscillograph,—all are scientific devices which have much to contribute to music education and are being used increasingly.

Added to these mechanical devices is a whole battery of scientifically constructed tests and measures covering native talent, musical achievement, and psychological reaction to music. A tremendous amount of research and experimentation is in progress and will warrant close scrutiny.

The Teacher. Be assured that no device, mechanical or otherwise, will replace either the studio or classroom music teacher. However, successful and effective school music teachers will need additional training and, in some areas, a different kind of training. There is a trend to extend the preparation of a school music teacher from four to five college years in an effort to increase the musicianship and general background definitely necessary to cope with present-day situations.

In the pedagogical phase of teacher education, stress is being placed increasingly upon the psychological and sociological outcomes of music instruction. In all music teaching, methods and techniques will need to be sought which will make the classroom a living example of a functioning democracy.

The Ignored or Forgotten Student. The United States Office of Education reveals that only twenty-five per cent of the students attending secondary schools are enrolled in some kind of music class or activity. Many high schools are trying to meet this deficiency by offering a course designed for the non-music student, called "Music for Living", "General Music", "Allied Arts", or "Fine Arts

4

Courses". This type of course serves a great need but taxes the ingenuity of the teacher as a broad background is an absolute essential.

The per cent of college students who have no contact with music of any kind is even larger than in the secondary school. This musically ignored group needs music as an essential part of a cultural education. There seems to be some hope of convincing college and university administrators that the study of applied music has laboratory value in validating theoretical and historical studies, and further, that their responsibility extends beyond the student registered in the music department, to include the entire student body.

America is experiencing a striking surge towards music. This is evidenced in many ways, for example; there are several hundred organized symphony orchestras with paid conductors in our country and even small towns have fine performing groups. Not until music has permeated the very fibre of the whole citizenry, individually and collectively, will the ultimate goal of music education be attained.

It is not too much to hope that the fine arts, and especially music, universally performed and understood, can be a fine and safe meeting place for friendship with the peoples of the whole world.

NOTE: More extended discussion of items suggested in this chapter will be found throughout the remainder of this book.

SECTION I

THE ELEMENTARY SCHOOL

Music practices in the elementary grades need to be brought into line with contemporary educational philosophies and techniques. A broad and basic concept of music, which includes self-expression and understanding through group activities as well as the development of skills, will lead to tolerance, emotional maturity, spiritual awareness, personal abilities, and a responsiveness to pattern and beauty.

A child's relationship with music as a skill and an art will result from a competent approach to the teaching of music in the elementary grades. It should be remembered always that early satisfactions and desires as well as actions and reactions, condition later growth and attitudes. However, the techniques used should never become larger nor more important than the thing taught, which in this case is music, nor should the thing taught be more important than the child.

PART I.
TECHNIQUES AND PROCEDURES IN THE ELEMENTARY SCHOOL

The six chapters which comprise Part I, deal with classroom organization and techniques for use with children from pre-school through the sixth grade. This material is based upon experience and general contemporary principles applied to school music teaching.

PART II.
ACTIVITIES AND ATTAINMENTS OF ELEMENTARY GRADES

It is recognized that levels of attainments and types of music activities will vary for many logical reasons. The four chapters which comprise Part II will aid in setting standards for the *average* school situation.

6

ELEMENTARY TEACHER PREPARATION AND GENERAL PRACTICES

Teaching is in reality a guidance program where the teacher directs the child along the educative path. It would follow that all school subjects, including music, should contribute to progress along this educative pathway and that all music activity should be purposeful in order to enhance this progress. Without doubt the teacher is the leader and balance-wheel in the educational program.

The Elementary Music Teacher

The successful teacher of music in the elementary grades needs to have as broad an academic and musical background as is possible in the training period. The training in music should include both vocal and instrumental phases. The extent of musical experiences should be such as to give the teacher a personal realization of the artistic, cultural, aesthetic, and spiritual values of music. A realization of the social significance of music coupled with a functioning knowledge of child psychology and a clear concept of the educational goal are imperative. Only those who enjoy a close and continued contact with small and growing children should aspire to be teachers in the elementary grades.

Physical Requirements. The minimum physical requirements for teaching music to children at the elementary grade level usually are considered as; (a) a pitch sense, so that the intonation of the tune will be correct; (b) a rhythmic sense, so that the flow of the music and the rhythmic patterns will be correct; and (c) an acceptable singing voice, so that songs presented by rote will be as near ideal as possible.

Pianistic Ability. The teacher, especially in the first three grades, needs to be able to play the piano sufficiently for the various music activities appropriate for these grades. After the children have learned to sing a song, an accompaniment played artistically adds to the aesthetic enjoyment. Recordings may be used advantageously to compensate for a deficiency in pianistic ability.

General Practices

The training, experience, and general intelligence of the teacher will be evident in the manner in which the classroom is organized and the general teaching techniques which are used.

Seating Arrangements. With the major attention directed to the development of the child, or in other words, what the music does for the child rather than what the child does for the music, traditional seating arrangements will need to be re-evaluated and adjusted in the light of the physical, social, and psychological needs of the individual child.

The early text books in the field of music education told us, "the monotones must be seated in the front of the room and those having leading and dependable voices, should occupy the rear seats. The remainder of the children would then be placed across the room between the monotones and the good singers. The names of birds or numbers may be used to identify the groups and this seating arrangement should always be followed."

The reasons for using this traditional group seating are scarcely acceptable in the light of present-day practices because the importance of the exceptions nullify its exclusive use. The reasons given for the traditional arrangements were briefly stated as follows: "(a) it seemed easier for the 'followers' to keep on pitch and follow the tune if the good voices were seated back of them, (b) the supervisor or music teacher who did not conduct the class regularly knew where to locate the good voices and could depend upon them to do individual or demonstration work correctly. Little or no difficulty was encountered in locating the unsteady voices for special help, (c) in general singing, the teacher conducting from the front of the room was in a position to help the poor singers with her own voice if she so desired."

It is granted that if the musical ability of the child was all that needed to be considered, there are no outstanding objections to an approximation of this traditional plan. However, such items as psychological reactions, physical comfort, and musical progress are of paramount importance and should take precedence over any arbitrary or traditional seating arrangement which is based entirely upon musical ability.

Sitting Position for Singing. Whenever the classroom situation will allow, it is advisable to have children stand when singing but it is recognized that many musical activities will need to take place while the children are seated. It should be satisfactory for any seated singing activity for a child to be in order, seated comfortably, and not in a strained position. A minimum of attention should be drawn to the feet, hands, back, chin, or any other part of the child's physical body, in order to avoid self-consciousness and take attention away from the music. The end-product of singing long phrases with proper breath support will tend automatically to elicit proper posture.

Tone Quality. One of the important objectives of all vocal music is good tone quality, so the elementary teacher needs to have a mental concept of the ideal tone which children are to produce. Furthermore, the teacher needs to be aware that the kind of tone quality which the children use will depend largely upon the quality of tone the teacher uses when singing for them. If joy and happiness are released through singing, the tone quality usually will be acceptable.

Most authorities agree that a light and free tone is desirable and natural for this age level of children. The tone should have life but should not be forced. When told to sing *softly,* a hushed, hooty, or covered quality is usually given, therefore, the use of the word *lightly,* is recommended. It is detrimental to both ears and vocal cords to require or permit the use of loud, forced, or raucous tones.

Tone quality is related to breath control but a natural breathing is ideal for the singing child, the only emphasis necessary is to give the child a feeling for the phrase unit of the song and to sing this phrase unit on one breath. If the teacher does this, the child will imitate and no discussion will be necessary.

Pitch. Because music is exact, it is advisable that songs be pitched correctly. The key note may be taken from an instrument or a pitchpipe and the beginning tone of the song in its turn taken from the key tone. This gives the singer the intonation of the key in which the song is written as well as the beginning tone of the selection.

Reasons For Pitch Variation

Any pitch which is not true has an undesirable effect upon the ears of the hearers. The variation may be above or below the true pitch but the latter is more common. There are many factors which affect the maintenance of correct pitch, some are unavoidable but others are within the control of the teacher. The cause should be investigated and removed if possible. Any of the following reasons may cause pitch variation.

1. Poor posture
2. Forced tones or singing too loudly
3. Fatigue

4. Too soon after eating
5. Several children with bad colds
6. Several cases of infected adenoids or tonsils
7. Too slow tempo
8. Improper tone production
9. Poor ventilation
10. One careless singer with a leading voice
11. Attention of the pupils not directed sufficiently toward maintaining the correct pitch.

All elementary teachers should be aware that an important part of teaching music is the development of pitch awareness on the part of the child. The ears must not only hear but the child should be pitch conscious at all times.

Tempo and Interpretation. Too slow a tempo or general speed in singing is a common criticism of all elementary school singing. A sprightly tempo is conducive to improved tone quality and avoids lesson drag. The text and music of the song should indicate the tempo to be used and the interpretation to be given. Children often make splendid suggestions for interpretation and their imagination and creativeness should be encouraged.

Individual Singing. Every child should be encouraged to sing alone from the beginning of his school life. The attitude of the teacher will determine the extent of the development of this individual confidence. If the child realizes early that to sing alone is no different from speaking alone he will have no difficulty with this activity. When a child makes a mistake or sings an incorrect note in music it should cause no more merriment or concern than when a mistake is made in addition or when a word is misspelled. Courtesy and cooperation will usually handle this situation.

The first individual singing should consist of songs that have been taught by rote. This, of course, does not take place until the song is well memorized by the entire class. Many methods of procedure may be followed, such as:

1. Children volunteer to sing alone
2. The teacher plans an impromptu program where children sing alone or in small groups
3. One child chooses another with whom to sing alternating phrases of a song
4. Begining in one part of the room, each child may take his turn in singing a phrase of a designated song.

In all singing, and especially individual singing, it should be remembered that if a child is paying close attention and is giving his best effort vocally, it should be accepted as such.

3

ROTE SONGS AND METHODS FOR PRESENTATION

Children are susceptible to songs sung for them and which they learn to sing by hearing. Songs which are learned by rote may be classified into (a) art songs, (b) observation songs, and (c) type or pattern songs, depending upon the purpose for which the song is taught.

The Need For Rote Songs

Singing should be one of the happiest experiences of any individual regardless of age. This is especially true of children in the elementary grades. If it is not true, the fault usually lies either in the material selected or the methods of presentation used by the teacher.

Definition. The word *rote* applies to the method used in learning the song rather than the song itself. A rote song is any song which is learned by hearing another sing it. That is, the song is not read from the printed page by the learner but is received by the ear, by imitation.

Art Songs. An art song is a rote song which is taught primarily for the aesthetic value derived, a song taught for the joy one gets from singing it and which has tested musical merit. The aesthetic desires of the child and his singing ability will often demand art songs which are greatly beyond his ability to read. Therefore, art songs taught to elementary school children may contain quite difficult rhythmic patterns and chromatic inflections because the children will not be expected to read them by note.

It is advisable to choose art songs for very small children which are not too long and with a range falling within the staff. As in all song literature, the words of the text should be within the comprehension of the child.

One of the best ways of integrating music into the life of a child and also with the other school subjects is through the use of art songs. Children love songs of nature and musical gems which deal with their home life and activities. In selecting art songs for children of any grade to sing, the teacher always should take into consideration the musical capacity of the child as an individual as well as the musical capacity of the class as a whole.

All art songs should possess qualities that are cultural because music used in a cultural way is as highly desirable and effective as literature or any of the other communicative arts. The study of gems of literature is begun in early childhood, likewise the gems of music should be used from the very beginning of a child's musical training and experience. For example, children enjoy singing lullabies, instead of using so many of the "little-girl-rocking-her-dolly" type, why not use such selections as *"Sweet and Low"* by Barnby and Brahms' *"Lullaby"*?

Inspiration plays a large part in the teaching of all music but this is especially true of art songs. If the teacher herself does not have an appreciation of and love for these musical gems, does not enjoy this contact and feel a thrill with the vibration of beautiful musical literature, she is not capable of calling forth the best from the child. If joy and cultural development are kept to the foreground, one can scarcely go amiss in the selection of art songs.

Observation Songs. An experience with oral words is necessary before a child is ready to begin the mastery of the written language. This also is true of music reading, therefore, an early visual experience with songs which have previously been learned by rote is a vital preface to the reading of printed music.

Children enjoy watching the printed page of a story while someone reads the words for them. They learn that words move along from left to right and soon identify repeated phrases or patterns of words. This is paralleled in the preliminary stages of reading music notation. Observation songs are simple songs which are taught by rote but which are contained in a book which is placed in the hands of each child. Definitely he is *not* reading either the words or the music but he is learning that music moves along from left to right, that certain characters called notes are high on the staff when his voice is high, and low on the staff when his voice is low. He learns that when his voice makes a wide skip in the tune, so do the notes, that when his voice stays on the same pitch or varies slightly, so do the notes.

No attempt should be made to have the children do anything with the mechanical details of the music of observation songs as the only purpose, and a tremendously important one, is that they get an over-all visual acquaintance with the printed music of the song.

Type or Pattern Songs. A type or pattern song is a rote song taught for the specific purpose of being used later as an aid in the mechanics of note reading. It is similar to an observation song in that it should be short, singable and contain a minimum of technical problems; rhythmic, melodic, or harmonic. It differs from an observation song in that it is necessary that a pattern or type song contain at least one of the following tonal patterns; octave skips, arpeggios, triads, repeated tones, and the diatonic scale either whole or in part. These tonal patterns may be in descending or ascending progression.

An ideal pattern song has only one stanza and should be selected from the book which will be in the hands of the child when he first begins to identify tonal patterns in his transition from rote (by ear) singing to note (by eye) reading.

The number of type or pattern songs necessary to make this transition may vary from ten to fifteen or twenty, depending upon the pattern content of the songs selected for this purpose.

Presentation of Rote Songs

A wide variety of methods for presenting songs by rote have been used successfully. These divide into two general classes, namely: (a) the full song method, and (b) the phrase method. In many instances it will be found desirable to use a "combined" method where part of the full song procedure is combined with a part of the phrase procedure.

The method selected for presenting song material by rote depends upon four items.

1. The ability of the children   3. The difficulty of the song
2. The ability of the teacher   4. The results desired.

The Full-Song Method. In using the full song method for presenting material to a class by rote, the teacher sings the song in its entirety for the children on several days preceding their participation. They become familiar with hearing the tune and learn how to say any outstanding words or words with which they are not familiar. They know what the song is telling them and any interesting items about the song.

The teacher may sing the song through a number of times while the attention of the class is directed to some specific word or idea. Further repetitions of the song may be made by the teacher as the children mark the rhythm with a wide swing of the arm or a touch of the hand on the desk. Any motion is permissible which gives a bodily feeling for the rhythmic flow of the music, is not violent, and does not make disturbing audible sounds.

The teacher may prove to herself that the class is familiar with the words by having the children "say the words with their lips" but not using their voices, while the teacher sings. It may be necessary to do this several times but the rather exaggerated movement of the lips tends to aid in correct enunciation. The children then sing the entire song while the teacher stands ready to help them by using her lips to form the words while the children are singing.

The end product of the full-song method is musical and smooth and does not waste time by needless piece-meal and uninteresting repetition.

The Phrase Method. This is a traditional method for rote song presentation and while it has some merit, the mechanical dissecting of a song is not conducive to child interest, economy of time, or musical flow. The following steps are used in the phrase by phrase presentation.

1. The teacher sings the entire song while the children listen. If there is more than one stanza, the first stanza should be repeated.
2. The teacher then sings the first phrase of the song being very careful to pronounce every word distinctly. The children listen.
3. The children sing the first phrase as sung in Step 2, by the teacher.
4. The teacher then sings the second phrase and the children repeat it after her. This process is continued until all phrases of the song are learned.
5. The teacher sings the entire song.
6. The pupils sing the entire song.

The Combined Method. Realizing that the method used in presenting songs by rote will influence the liking a child has for a particular song and may affect his basic attitude toward all music, many teachers begin their rote song presentation with the full-song approach and only where difficulty is encountered, is the phrase isolated and repeated to insure correctness. Following this isolation of a phrase for drill purposes, the phrase is replaced immediately by the singing of the song in its entirety.

Recognizing that the ultimate goal is that the class can sing the song in tune, with proper regard for tempo and dynamics and a comprehension of the thought content, the efficient teacher will devise a combined method of presentation which will be effective and economical for use with a specific group of children.

The Selection of Rote Song Material

Some fundamental items concerning the selection of rote song material in addition to those already stated under the headings of art songs, observation songs, and type or pattern songs, should be considered as the selection of the material to be presented by rote in the elementary grades stands on a par in importance with the method of presenting such material.

Children should do beautiful things, see beautiful things, hear beautiful things, and sing beautiful things. The child has an inborn sense of beauty and he is, by nature, anxious to sing songs if they are beautiful, interesting, and within his ability to perform.

The text of the song as well as the music should be carefully investigated to assure that the rhythmic flow and tune line of the music conform with and enhance the mood and thought expressed by the text. The text should be suitable in thought and word content for the grade level where it is used. The music should be interesting but not too difficult for the grade level, should have sufficient musical merit so that it is worthy of memorization by the children.

The attitude of the group, including thoughts, feelings, and reactions may be influenced greatly by the singing activity provided the music is properly selected. It should be remembered that acknowledged or standard composers and recognized folk songs are valuable sources for excellent rote song material.

4

SINGING AND REMEDIAL PRACTICES

Vocal utterance is the first tonal experience of the child. It is normal and natural for a satisfied and happy child to make vocal sounds. These vocal tones will vary in pitch and so become a singing experience. Speech readiness and singing readiness occur almost simultaneously. The principles underlying the acquirement of oral speech apply equally well to the acquirement of singing songs. The basis in both instances is *imitation*.

Singing should be regarded as a learning-art activity and singing should result in a pleasurable experience which gives an ability to express ideas and feelings through song. Young children should have many songs sung to them because they are highly imitative and learn quickly by rote.

As the singing of rote songs is an important part of all elementary grade music, Chapter III was devoted entirely to the selection of rote song material and the various methods used in the presentation of songs to be learned by imitation. Certain normal individual needs become apparent immediately when the child tries to sing.

Individual Needs

Practically all phases of individual differences appear in the individual vocal needs of elementary school children. There are differences in previous musical experience, in musical interest, in emotional stability, as well as differences in vocal ability. All elementary teachers and especially those teaching below the fourth grade, need to be able to cope with these varied situations. Vocal limitations should be approached with understanding and certainly not with awe, fear, or irritation.

Suggested Individual Classification. No work in individual singing should be begun until the child has become thoroughly adjusted to his surroundings and the class as a whole has acquired a repertoire or ten or twelve songs. The teacher can then readily classify the voices into four groupings *for her own information*. The data for this classification should be acquired in an informal manner such as tonal imitations, singing conversations, games and dramatic play, as well as by listening to individual children while the entire class is singing. The groupings are:

1. Those who are capable of singing
2. Followers
3. Absolute monotones
4. Conversational singers

Capable Singers

These children generally have had experience in singing songs and have developed a feeling for pitch and rhythm. As soon as the children in this group have a concept of the right kind of tone quality to use, the principal thing they need is an enlarged repertoire of songs and plenty of opportunity to sing.

Followers

A child is classified as a follower when he can sing the song correctly as long as the teacher or some student with a dependable voice sings with him but who cannot maintain the song if singing alone. This child needs encouragement to establish confidence in his own ability and any feeling of failure should be avoided. The emphasis should be placed upon the using of his ears to listen carefully before he tries to sing as well as while he is singing.

Usually all that is needed by a *follower* is time for him to have sufficient experience with singing. It has been found helpful to seat a *follower* directly in front of a dependable voice or better still, to seat him between two such voices.

Absolute Monotones

The term "monotone" is used improperly to describe children who have not learned as yet, to carry a tune in singing. An absolute monotone is a child who sings on one pitch only and never varies from that one pitch. This is very rare, perhaps one in a thousand and is generally due to physical handicaps either in the throat or the ear. The advice of the school physician should be sought. This child should not be excluded from the singing activity unless the physician so advises.

Conversational Singers

A conversational singer is one who inflects his voice as he does in speaking with no regard for tune line. His problem is one of pitch but a rhythmic sense also may be lacking. A conversational singer needs experience in trying to sing and also needs special attention.

About one-half of the children entering the average kindergarten belong to this group. The most outstanding reason for this large number of tuneless little folk is that no one has taken the time to help them find themselves vocally. This duty falls to the lot of the primary teacher and should be considered a privilege and not a task. It is a thrilling experience to realize that *you* have put the power to sing into the life of an individual, for if one can give to a child the power of song, one has given him something that money cannot buy and which will be his as long as he lives.

As every child has the right to sing, or to attempt to sing, a monotone or a conversational singer should not be told to keep still and only rarely should he be told to keep still and listen. He should be encouraged to sing with a 'little voice' or 'like a fairy' and listen while he sings. He should try to match his voice with the rest of the class. If he gives his best, it should be accepted as such. He will soon be able to help himself if he is taught to use his ears.

The minute a child is convinced that he *cannot* sing, it is almost impossible to help him. Unfortunately, he is often told this at home and perhaps his attempts at singing have been laughed at. This makes it doubly difficult for the teacher as well as the child.

When the singing difficulty has arisen from faulty listening habits, the child is eliminated generally from the conversational-singer class during the first school year. Such troubles should never be allowed to progress as high as the third or fourth grade for at that age level children become too self-conscious. Some few cases are due to chronic throat trouble and on a physician's advice, this child should not be allowed to sing.

Suggested Aids. Many devices have been used successfully for helping children to find their singing voices. An alert teacher will originate others which are related to the specific situation. Many songs have octaves, arpeggios, and repeated tones which are very helpful when isolated and used for drill purposes.

Theoretically, the teacher should begin with a high pitched tone and proceed downward thus carrying the head tone quality down Pedagogically, the teacher must begin with the tone the child has and work from that either upward or downward as the case may be. This is making use of the common sense practice of going from the known to the related unknown. It should be remembered that tone quality can be developed after the pitch is firmly established.

Humming a sustained tone, first as a class and then as individuals, is all that is necessary in many cases. If the child cannot match a

18

given tone, have him come near you and "use his ears" while you hum the pitch again for him.

One of the first pitches which a child should be asked to match is E located in the fourth space of the treble clef. After matching the high tone, have the pupils match E located on the first line in the treble clef.

Any classroom teacher of average ability should be able to locate her most difficult cases in a very short time. These little folk who have not located their voices as yet may be kept toward the front of the group in order to receive help more readily unless there are physical, psychological, or sociological reasons for not doing so. Some examples of conversational singer helps are given.

EXAMPLES

1. The teacher calls the child's name

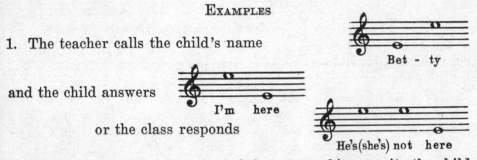

Bet - ty

and the child answers

I'm here

or the class responds

He's(she's) not here

This reversal of the direction of the octave skip permits the child to match the teacher's last tone before attempting to sing his octave interval.

2. The teacher sings a question

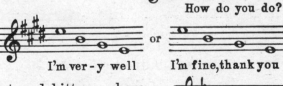

How do you do?

and the child answers   or

I'm ver - y well   I'm fine, thank you

3. There is a game of cat and kittens where the mother cat says

Me - ow

and the baby cat says

Me - ow

The children will enjoy guessing which kind of a cat each member of the class is representing.

4. The teacher pretends she is playing a violin and makes the motions of drawing the bow down or up across the strings. The children watch closely and hum the descending or ascending octave as the teacher indicates the direction with her imaginary bow.

5. The children may make the motion of playing a slide trombone while humming or singing a descending octave.

6. While imitating the playing of the snare drum, the children may

sing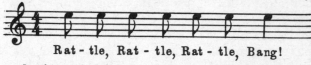

Rat - tle, Rat - tle, Rat - tle, Bang!

and while imitating the playing of the bass drum, the children may

sing

Boom! Boom! Boom! Boom!

Numbers four, five and six above are helpful in familiarizing the children with various musical instruments, with the singing seemingly incidental.

7. The dramatization of the story of the "Cow and the Train" has many concomitant learnings. - - - An old cow was going out for a walk one day. Because cows do not go to school, she didn't know that the safest way to cross a railroad track was to look first to the right and then to the left and if she saw no train coming, she would hurry right across the track.

Sure enough on her walk she came to a railroad track and without looking to either side, she walked right out to the middle of the track and stopped. She put her nose way out like cows do and said

Mo - oo!

Of course the man in the engine saw her and he didn't want to hurt

her so he made the train whistle say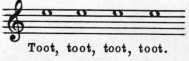

Toot, toot, toot, toot.

The cow heard the whistle but she didn't know that when you hear a horn honk or a whistle toot you should look around and be careful

so she just stretched her nose out and said

Mo - oo! Mo - oo!

By that time the train was getting very close so the whistle gave

one long

Too - oo - oo - oot.

The cow was frightened and ran home as fast as she could. But the next time she went for a walk and came to a railroad track she always stopped, looked both ways, and then if no train was coming, she walked right across.

8. Strange as it may seem, a minor interval will often reach some voices. A number of street calls use the "do - la" interval, a descending minor third. An interesting game can be made by the teacher telling of an old man driving down the street with a wagon full of vegetables and fruits which are good for girls and boys to eat. The children are asked to think of something which he might have to sell.

Then the teacher asks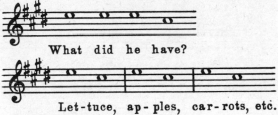

What did he have?

and as she passes around among the children they answer individually

Let-tuce, ap-ples, car-rots, etc.

This game may be adapted to playing that the children are in a restaurant or cafe and are ordering things from the menu.

9. The newsboy game is a favorite. At first the teacher is the newsboy and then a competent child may take the part. Each child holds his hand closed on top of his desk as if he were holding a coin. The

newsboy then starts his round calling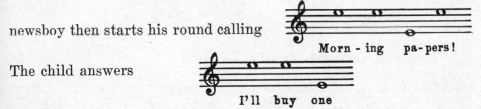

Morn - ing pa-pers!

The child answers

I'll buy one

The pretend coin is given to the newsboy who puts it in his pocket. The child who has just made the purchase puts his hands in his lap thus signifying that he has had his turn.

10. The imitation of church bells is interesting especially if a church is located near the school and the ringing of the bell can be heard.

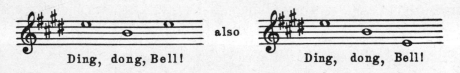

Ding, dong, Bell!   also   Ding, dong, Bell!

11. If the children have heard a siren whistle or the sound of a fire engine bell, then use

The siren should be done with a gradual slur upward with the last tone being held. This is a practical conversational singer aid because one can begin with the tone the child has and slide the voice upward as far as he can, however, the octave interval is recommended.

12. Children enjoy bird calls similar to the following:

13. The game of "guess who" is played by blindfolding one child.

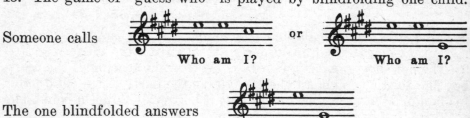

The one blindfolded answers

If he is correct, the class answers

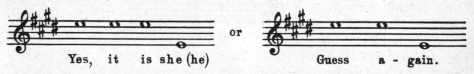

An alert teacher will find many times during the day in classes other than the singing period when these little devices can be used. It should be remembered that no one device or help or idea will fill all needs or accomplish all purposes for all children. It will be necessary to try many new things and re-try old ones many times before all children will be eliminated from the conversational singer group. It should be remembered, also, that *very* short practice periods and incidental attention bring best results.

5

INSTRUMENTAL MUSIC ACTIVITIES IN THE ELEMENTARY SCHOOL

Rhythmic development and muscular coordination brought about by games and dances form a basis for instrumental training and are often begun in the home. These so-called 'incidental experiences' are usually followed by experimentation with picking out tunes on the piano and with simple types of melodic-precussion instruments such as chimes, bells, and xylophone.

Children should be encouraged to play on the piano the tunes which they have learned to sing because there is considerable educative value in developing rhythmic and melodic sense by familiarity with a space-frame instrument. This familiarity with the keyboard is considered a fundamental prerequisite to the introduction of the child to the playing of standard musical instruments.

The instrumental activities conducted in the elementary grades will depend in the main upon the interest and instrumental ability of the classroom teacher, the presence of private teachers in the community, and the availability of instruments. A fine instrumental organization in the local junior or senior high school is a great incentive to instrumental activity in the lower grades.

Rhythm bands, instrumental ensembles, piano and other instrument classes, as well as all-school orchestras and bands are to be found in most elementary schools.

Rhythm Bands. Interest in the rhythm band has been continuing since the advent of the "Kindersymphonie" by Haydn, written in the latter part of the eighteenth century. Percussion instruments used in the primary grades are usually the first contact a child has with active participation in producing instrumental music. His singing, listening, and rhythmic experiences naturally lead into the rhythm band activity.

In addition to muscular coordination and the introduction to participation in instrumental music, the educational values can be stated briefly as: a realization of tempo and dynamics, a feeling for accented and unaccented beats, active and alert listening, contact with music literature, and appropriateness of instrumental tone quality to the mood of music. Advanced rhythm band work calls for printed music, or better still, music written by the children, and involves the knowledge of note and rest values.

Suggested Instrumentation

A well balanced rhythm band would contain the following commercially made instruments. The number of balance is indicated in parenthesis but various substitutions may be desirable.

Sticks (8 or 12 pairs)
Drum (bass, snare, or both)
Bells (turkey bells on a strap or tree bells)
Triangles (2)
Woodblock (1)
Tambourines (2)
Cymbals (1 pair crash, 1 single for gong)
Jingle Sticks (2)
Sand Blocks (2)
Bird Whistles (2)
Castanets (1 on a stick)
Tom-tom (1)
Xylophone (1)

Simple home-made or improvised instruments are quite satisfactory and many profitable hand-work projects may be developed. An ingenious teacher will be able to provide additions to the following suggestions.
1. Drums made from coffee or oatmeal boxes with rubber from inner tubes for drum heads
2. Blocks of wood covered with sandpaper
3. Pieces of iron or steel that have pleasing tones, suspended by a cord and struck with a large nail
4. Violins made from cigar boxes
5. Cymbals from lids or covers
6. Paper horns
7. Tambourines from paper plates with bells or buttons fastened on the edge
8. Pebbles in a tin can for a rattle

Leadership

Several leaders or conductors should be chosen as ability is demonstrated. They may carry out such conducting activities as holding the hands up for attention, outlining the beat with a baton, motioning for certain instruments when it is time for their particular part, indicating loud and soft passages, a down beat for starting, a cut-off beat for stopping, and a bow to the audience at the end of the selection.

EXAMPLE OF MUSIC FOR RHYTHM ORCHESTRA

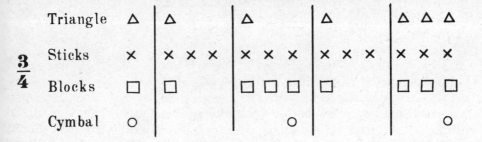

EXAMPLE OF PICTURE MUSIC FOR RHYTHM ORCHESTRA

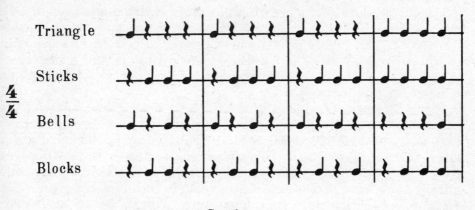

Caution

Rhythm bands have considerable audience appeal and some tendency for over-exploitation has been noted. This immediately defeats the basic learning purpose of the activity especially if the work has been done under dictation by the teacher and not developed by pupil-teacher planning.

In no instance should this percussive rhythm activity become simply a 'banging' or 'rattling' with no attention paid to the details of the music nor the appropriateness of the sound.

Pre-Orchestral Instruments. There are two major kinds of pre-orchestral instruments, percussion and melody. The percussion instruments are a continuation of those used in the rhythm band but should include written music for note reading and the beginning of snare drum technique. The only equipment necessary for this percussive training is a pair of drum sticks and a practice pad. The melody producing instruments are simple wind instruments of the flageolet, tonette, flutophone, or recorder type.

Most music educators agree that the third grade is the approximate level where the use of elementary instruments can be introduced most advantageously. These instruments serve four major purposes in musical development.

1. Talent finders
2. Development of ensemble awareness
3. Development of melodic feeling
4. Opportunity for note reading

It is considered far better to make a small investment in preliminary instruments than for parents to buy a standard instrument and then discover that their child lacks the ability or interest to master the instrument. Unless the entire class is supplied with instruments some child with outstanding talent and potentialities may be overlooked.

The advantages of the use of exploratory instruments are: (a) the cost is low, (b) they are simple in construction and are relatively easy to play, and (c) grade teachers can quickly learn to teach children how to play them. If a child shows interest and a degree of aptitude, he should be given guidance and encouraged to choose an instrument for further study.

Piano Classes. The piano is considered a basic instrument for the presentation of all the fundamentals of music. Piano classes have been successful as low as the second grade, however the third grade is considered more ideal. Beginning piano classes should be open to all children for exploratory purposes with intermediate and advanced classes for those making adequate technical progress. The teacher instructing this group not only should be an acceptable pianist but be trained in piano class teaching techniques.

Experience has shown that the study of piano, if begun at an early age, builds a firm musical foundation for further study before the child becomes involved with other extra-curricular activities. The mastery of technical and reading skills, including the development of musicianship, thereby parallels his mental development in his other scholastic studies, resulting in a greater continuity of interest.

Instrumental Classes. If a foundation in piano is acquired in grades three and four along with experience with pre-orchestra or exploratory instruments, children are ready for instruction on most of the major instruments.

Many children will have progressed sufficiently by the end of one semester of class lessons to be acceptable members of the elementary band or orchestra. It is unwise to enroll unprepared students in these large ensembles, therefore advanced instrumental technique classes should be available so that the beginner may progress with the playing of his chosen instrument until he is sufficiently proficient to be an asset to the band or orchestra.

Instrumental classes may be organized according to two plans and each plan has its advantages.
1. All members are players of similar instruments, that is, classes for woodwinds, brass, or strings.
2. All members are at approximately the same level of proficiency regardless of the kind of instrument.

Some authorities recommend that students choose one of three basic instruments, cornet, clarinet, or violin, and after the initial technique has been mastered, a change-over is made to an instrument which is less common and for which the child has demonstrated an aptitude.

Instrumental class instruction should be in the hands of an acceptable performer on the instruments taught, who know teaching techniques and has a working knowledge of child psychology.

Ensembles. After one semester of beginning class work has been successfully completed, students should be grouped into small ensembles. This encourages additional practice, affords acquaintance with ensemble literature and leads to greater independence and general musicianship of the players. Many elementary schools do not have sufficient instruments for a band or orchestra and would profit greatly by small ensemble organizations.

Bands and Orchestras. Some elementary school bands and orchestras are in reality only enlarged ensembles which make use of available players and this is as it should be. Only the larger elementary schools will have sufficient capable instrumental players to form a balanced orchestra or band. However, after proper stress has been placed upon beginning instrument classes and small ensembles, the organization of an elementary school band and orchestra should be encouraged.

It should be rememebered that instrumental music is an integral part of the elementary school music program and should not be regarded as a special activity planned especially for the unusually talented few. The ultimate accomplishmnt of the entire instrumental program in all schools regardless of grade level, is dependent to a large degree upon the success of the teaching of the fundamentals of playing the instrument. To handle this beginning work in classes is a democratic way to make the opportunity available for all. Often the educative values are quite as great for ordinary players with simple instruments as it is for a very talented player with a difficult instrument.

6 LISTENING AS A PART OF MUSIC EDUCATION

The word *appreciation* as applied to any of the arts has had many definitions. It concerns a large area and the facets are numerous and vary with individuals, with situations, and with materials. While this chapter will be concerned chiefly with listening as an elementary school activity, it must be remembered that music appreciation, of which listening is an important part, embraces all music education activities.

Listening should be regarded as a skill as well as an art because skillful listening is in reality a form of ear-training. Music listening is not only an absorption process but needs to be directed, practiced, and learned.

Listening Experiences. The kinds of listening experiences may be stated briefly as follows.

1. Listening to songs in order to learn the words and music.

2. Listening to instrumental music for rhythmic expression.

3. Listening to recorded or "live" music for, (a) the pleasure it affords, (b) contact and acquaintance with musical literature, (c) understanding and recognition of musical form, (d) development of discrimination and critical evaluation, (e) knowledge of great personalities in music, both past and present, and an understanding of the historic period in which they lived.

The occasions for the listening experiences are to be found both during and outside of school hours and fall roughly into six classes, namely: (a) listening while performing, (b) listening while others perform, (c) listening to the playing of recordings, (d) listening to the radio, (e) listening while watching television, and (f) listening while watching sound motion pictures. (See Chapters IX, X, and XI.)

Active Listening. Active listening is purposeful listening. It might be based upon the story which the composer has told in music, such as *"Of a Tailor and a Bear"* by MacDowell; or the identification of a tune, as found in the *"Rondino"* by Kreisler on a Beethoven theme; or the recognition of changes of tempo as in *"Badinage"* by Herbert; or the identification of certain instruments (violin and 'cello), as in *"The Invitation to the Waltz"* by Weber. Active listening is always alert listening whether it be directed or undirected by the teacher.

28

It is not only legitimate but very desirable to have occasions when children listen to music for the sheer enjoyment of contact with loveliness. This would mean no visible participation on the part of the child, no discussion nor direction, no answers requested to questions but simply quiet absorption. This so-called passive listening may be used for rest purposes, to relieve tension, or purely for personal enjoyment.

The Teacher. An adequate background for the successful teaching of music appreciation would include a broad general education not only in music but in all the fine arts.

Such self-expressive activities as song singing, instrument playing, rhythmics including dancing, and the writing of original melodies should be encouraged by the teacher because these require active listening and develop an appreciation and understanding of the music involved.

At times it may be necessary to supply information as a background to facilitate listening and so the teacher will need to have an adequate knowledge of materials and techniques for presentation. But most important of all, the elementary teacher must have an enthusiasm based upon a personal love for and enjoyment of music. There is nothing more contagious than enthusiastic delight.

The Child. The child in the elementary grades should have opportunity to experience much music of all kinds for purposes of exploration and pleasure. However, the music should change progressively with his power to enjoy, his changing musical standards, and his development in appreciation.

The child should not be dominated by suggestions or indications of rightness or wrongness *before* he hears the music for the first time as it is considered best for his first impressions to be entirely his own and based upon how *he* hears the music and the meaning it has for *him*. His opinions and reactions can be contrasted and compared later with those of other members of the class. This may take place orally or through bodily response. The child should not be forced to accept interpretations of the teacher or even the majority of the class but rather on a basis of judgment, with choice and freedom of expression based on honest discrimination. Judicial guidance and repeated hearings may or may not align him with the majority reaction.

Techniques. Usually the music should be enjoyed as a whole, as a musical experience, before any factual material is presented to the students. Analysis or information should be given only when it will enhance the scope of the over-all appreciation of the music heard. It should not be necessary to improvise unreal or imaginary stories to make music appealing. In most listening at the elementary level, the purely theoretical aspects should be kept at a minimum because they are unnecessary at this stage of development and are largely beyond the comprehension of the child. This is especially true in the primary grades.

As the child learns to recognize and produce tonal patterns, rhythmic patterns, dynamics, and form in the songs he sings, he transfers this ability to his active listening. Selections need to be re-heard many times so that the attention may be centered upon one thing at each hearing. These items, once identified, may be combined at subsequent hearings. Indiscriminate playing for pupils is usually a poor technique as the purpose for listening should be clear to the child.

A logical starting place for the selection of music for a listening project for small children is to choose material so that it is within the scope of interest and capacity for understanding of the group. The first appeal will be rhythmic, followed in turn by melodic and harmonic interest. Young children grow impatient with long selections so it is advisable to choose short ones with clearly marked characteristic rhythms. The melody should be easy to follow and if a song, the words need to be understood.

One of the finest techniques for the integration of pre-note reading with listening is to have the books in the hands of the primary children so that they may watch the printed page of music while they hear the songs sung by the teacher, from recordings, or while they sing the songs which they have previously learned by rote. (See Chapter IX. This can be carried higher in the intermediate grades to enhance the idea of 'so it looks, so it sounds'.

The basic techniques for listening divide into two classes according to purpose, (a) those which help in 'learning to listen', and (b) those which help in 'listening to learn'. If the music suggests activity, expresses mood, feeling or emotion, or tells a story, it is generally classified as an aid in learning to listen and accounts for the major portion of the activities in the primary grades. The natural curiosity of the child will carry him over into the 'listening to learn' of new things which will be provided for him in the intermediate grades. Recently published music text books in various series have recorded song material and directions for the listening activity.

In addition to the listening aspects of the every-day music class, schools should take the initiative in providing opportunities for elementary children to hear fine music artistically performed so that standards may be established and musical taste developed. This would indicate high calibre concerts by local or visiting professional musicians from solo performers to complete symphonies giving programs especially designed for children. It also could mean the encouragement or sponsoring of certain radio and television time where concerts for school listening would be scheduled.

Fundamental Principles. Listening should not be isolated as a special activity in the elementary grades, rather it should permeate the entire music program. Guidance is necessary in listening as in all other learning processes. Good listening habits can be established if the techniques and materials are suited to the experience level of the hearer.

The ability of an individual to listen intelligently and to experience an appreciation of what is heard does not depend upon his ability or non-ability to actually perform the music himself. Because the child is too young to understand the technical analysis of a musical selection is no reason to suppose that he cannot thrill with the beauty of tone, structure, etc., even though he does not and can not understand why at this time.

While it is advisable to plan a logical and desirable sequence for music listening activities, it should be remembered that levels of appreciation are not common even to all pupils of any one grade level, — the important thing is that the teacher has a clear concept of the desired goals and values as they apply to each individual child.

Elementary Grade Attainments. All attainments in listening depend largely upon initial contacts and repetitions which have been properly guided. If the hearing of music has been an active phase of all music participation at all grade levels, children will have achieved the following as minimum listening abilities during the elementary grades.

1. A freeness in using known rhythmic activities for the interpretation of new music heard. This would demonstrate a resourcefulness for rhythmic self-expression and indicate an interest in the dramatization of both instrumental and vocal music.
2. A recognition of the rhythmic patterns of such dance tunes as the polka, gavotte, schottische, and waltz, based on the experience of having danced the various steps.
3. An ability to recognize themes heard from standard musical selections as well as to identify some selections by title and composer when heard on the radio, television, at concerts, or elsewhere.
4. A realization that melodic changes add to the beauty of music by increasing the interest and variety, and also the ability to recognize some of the more obvious alterations in the melodies heard.
5. An awareness that the spirit and mood portrayed by music can be expressed likewise through pictures and other art media.
6. An awareness of the unique tone quality of the various symphonic instruments and an ability to identify each by both sight and sound.
7. A sincere enjoyment of and reaction to lovely and beautiful music.

Summary. Sixth grade children, through cumulative experience, will have developed an active interest in hearing music. They will have acquired the fundamentals of intelligent listening, a knowledge of musical compositions by the great masters, and an ability to analyze for form of construction. They will know instruments by sight and sound, individually and in combination. They will have matured sufficiently to identify and follow the ways in which music expresses action, story, design, and mood; and they should be more discriminating of music heard at concerts, over the air, on recordings and at motion pictures.

All this should guarantee pleasurable listening for these children during years spent in the junior and senior high school and for all years to come.

7 THE CREATIVE ACTIVITY

Because creative potentialities are present in all phases of music education at all grade levels and in all types of activities, the reader will find numerous references to creative activities throughout this book. As a basic concept of creative education is vitally important, this chapter merits a place in the over-all music education program.

Present day educators agree that creative expression by the child, especially in the arts, makes a major contribution toward the maximum development of the individual. A lack of specific definition of what constitutes a creative activity and variance of procedures have resulted in considerable confusion. If Hockett's* definition is accepted, a major portion of the activities of the entire school day will contain some elements of creativeness. He believes that any work which has the quality of originality, ingenuity, inventiveness, experimentation, uniqueness, initiative, freshness, newness, or change, is creative for that individual to some degree at least.

The Creative Teacher. There always have been creative teachers, that is, those who have challenged the initiative and imagination of the child, and such a teacher always has used creative activities to further the development of children. A well prepared and alert teacher is the focal point around which the creative concept of education moves and such a teacher will understand each individual child and will immediately win confidence and respect. This will lead to self-confidence on the part of the child and a realization of the value of his individual contribution.

A creative teacher will know when guidance is necessary and even more important, will know when to withhold it. In order to aid the child in developing standards which are in accordance with the grade level, kindly criticism and direction will need to be given. This should not be simply an imposition of adult standards but rather the use of the strong social influence of the class functioning as an evaluating audience. The ultimate goal of any creative teaching is the development of wholesome and integrated personalities, as well as a furtherance of skills, techniques, and knowledge.

*Hockett, John A. "The Significance of Creative Expression," California Journal of Education, 9:159–165. February, 1941.

Self analysis by teachers who are not creative in their attitudes or techniques reveals that they feel a lack of training in both the theory and methods for teaching creatively. They are self-conscious and unable to cope with large projects. Many special music teachers fail to utilize the creative impulse when the occasion arises because they are not familiar sufficiently with all the daily activities of the various elementary grades.

The Child. Any situation which calls forth an especially significant or new response from the child is, for him, a creative activity. Even though only a very few can produce great creations, all children have creative potentialities to some degree provided they are surrounded by a rich and stimulating school environment and not hampered by dominating direction. It has been demonstrated that the outcome of creative teaching will be the creative development of the child.

The forward view of education holds discovery and formulation of concepts for future use by the child without neglecting the past with its implications for the present and future. The creative approach produces a happy child in an agreeable situation where things are happening and he is important and independent.

The Projects or Activities. It is granted that real and functional situations are the most vital for the development of special abilities and skills. Maximum educational values result from voluntary participation in cooperative and creative activities. Any significant situation which challenges the interest of the child and provides opportunity for him to advance is a proper creative activity. This does not suggest the elimination of all guidance on the part of the teacher but challenges the teaching technique used. The pupil-teacher relationship in any creative project if it is to be successful, must be one of friendly helpfulness.

A flexible curriculum is a great asset to creative activities as it allows freedom and gives additional time for individuals and groups who are interested and working to continue until a logical stopping place is found. This asset of freedom should not be abused to the detriment of any area of the school day but a wise teacher can equalize the program in the light of longer-span accomplishment.

Certain types of equipment need to be available for creative use in all elementary schools such as recordings, teacher and pupil reference books, pictures, and manuscript paper. A phonograph, piano, and radio should be available as well as rhythm and melody instruments. It must be remembered however, that children are resourceful and improvised materials often give best results.

No creative project should be superimposed but should be a natural outgrowth and have a definite, logical relationship. For example, instead of the teacher announcing that, "Today we are going to make drums," and then proceeding to tell or show the class just how and what to do, a discussion of primitive man, the early beginnings of music, or some phases of social studies may lead to an interest *in* and an incentive *for* the children to try their hands at making drums of various kinds. This project may be very simple and of short duration depending upon the continued interest and need which the children have. Or it may involve research, the study of rhythmic patterns, the effects of size and materials upon the tone quality produced, and lead to the writing of original rhythmic accompaniments for primitive songs.

There is no *best* set of directions for carrying on a creative activity in music because its very nature makes this undesirable. A few suggestions may prove helpful in indicating possibilities.

In the singing of a song or the playing of a musical selection, the performer re-creates the work of the composer and he combines his own emotional tone and interpretation of the meaning with that of the composer. Dramatization and original dance interpretation of instrumental and vocal selections give added meaning and life. A simple bodily response to rhythmic patterns or the chanting of a line of poetry may develop into a tune line which is entirely original. Tune writing is a gradual development of musical imagination, ideas, and skills which are based upon a feeling by the child of the legitimacy of his freedom to express himself.

In the primary grades it is necessary for the teacher to be able to write the music her class originates if it is to be preserved but the children in the intermediate grades will feel need for a knowledge of notation so they may write down the tunes which they have created. They may desire to add a harmony part for a second voice to sing or an instrument to play.

It is important to remember in original song writing by children that the end product is not the all-important thing because according to standards which make musical selections endure, only a very, very small number would merit consideration. While it is proper to strive for acceptability with perfection as a goal, the important educational outcome of any creative activity is what the participation in the activity has done *for* and *to* the individual who has participated in the creating.

The rhythm band (See Chapter V, page 23.) affords a rich opportunity for originality along with the awareness of a feeling for rhythmic patterns, accent and phrasing; as well as a discrimination for changes in tempo, intensity and duration. A discussion and evaluation of the suitability of certain rhythm instruments for specific musical interpretation leads to creative thinking. For example, the children have heard a recorded selection and the problem is how to interpret it with the available rhythm instruments. The children will need to decide many things such as which instrument should play on the accented beats, which on the unaccented, which should play at the climax, which ones serve best when only used occasionally for special effects, and whether or not the instrumentation should be changed if theme is repeated. Many of these items will be decided upon a basis of experimentation and an expression of preference by the entire class.

Creative listening to music involves the encouragement of the child to make honest judgments and evaluations of his own musical productions as well as to all the music he hears. The discovery by a child that a theme recurs, that certain instruments are playing, that the tempo changes, that there is form and pattern in music based upon contrast and repetition, sets up new standards for future evaluations and judgments and gives him a concept of what he may incorporate in any writing he may do. It is not uncommon for the hearing of certain musical selections to stimulate the painting of a picture, the devising of dance steps, or the writing of a poem. If the listening to music causes the hearer to think and to feel, it is for him creative listening.

Evaluation. It is well to remember in evaluating any creative project that while the thing which is created should be commended if it has artistic value, the real measure of achievement which is appropriate and proper for any creative project or activity at the elementary grade level is the growth and development of the child.

NURSERY SCHOOL, PRE-SCHOOL, AND KINDERGARTEN

Increasing attention is being given by parents, psychologists, and educators to the area of childhood education which precedes his entrance to the first grade of school. Much truth has been found in the old adage that 'as a twig is bent, so is the tree inclined'. It has been proved that interests, habits, skills, and tendencies have their roots in very early childhood.

Reasons for Attendance. There are two major reasons why children attend school at an earlier age than required or permitted by school law. The *first* and ideal reason is for educational purposes. Many children have physical energy coupled with demonstrated abilities and interests which are recognized by parents, and upon testing are found to be older mentally than their chronological age. Some parents are financially able to pay tuition so that their children may have this early training and experience. The *second* reason is economic pressure in the home where it is necessary for the child to be cared for while the mother is engaged in remunerative duties. The child of the gainfully employed mother may not possess the physical development, interest, and abilities to profit to the maximum from pre-school attendance but it is expedient for him to attend. Regardless of what the reason for attendance is, the educational objectives for this early schooling may be briefly stated as follows.

1. To establish good habits including social adjustment which can facilitate and open up for the child the art of living.

2. To afford instruction commensurate with the capacity of the child.

Types of Schools. Maturation takes place rapidly in very young children. There is much difference in the amount of physical attention a child needs at one year and at three years of age. The activities of children who are age three vary in many respects from the child of five. It must be remembered, also, that there may be considerable difference between the mental age as well as the chronological age of any child so there is a need for varying types of schools.

For many years the term "kindergarten" was used indiscriminately for all pre-schools. However, there are four distinct types of schools which children may attend prior to entering the first grade. These are: (a) child-care school, (b) nursery school, (c) junior kindergarten, and (d) senior kindergarten.

Child-Care School

The primary purpose of the child-care school is to care for the physical needs of children between the ages of one and four years. These schools make little or no pretense of having an educational program. This school is often called a child-care center because they usually are located in thickly populated areas where play space is limited and where there are many working mothers who need to leave their small children in reliable hands.

The persons in charge of such schools should have training in nursing but also should have preparation in recreational activities for young children. In addition to the many personal qualifications, an agreeable speaking and singing voice, the ability to play the piano, and a knowledge of educational techniques and materials are very advantageous for one employed in a child-care school.

Nursery School

Most nursery schools enroll children below four years of age and have a definite educational program and are equipped to carry on educational activities. Nursery schools are often located in thickly populated or industrial areas but they will be found also in substantial sections of larger cities.

While a trained nurse is included on the staff of most nursery schools, the personnel is composed largely of teachers who have made a study of child psychology and introductory teaching methods.

Junior and Senior Kindergarten

The junior kindergarten is distinguished from the senior kindergarten largely in terms of age level, the junior kindergarten is for four year old children and the senior kindergarten cares for the five year olds. These kindergartens both have well planned educational programs and are usually well equipped. The staff is composed of trained kindergarten teachers with perhaps a visiting nurse available. Many local school systems have had classes for five year old children for many years, usually organized as a separate unit from the elementary school and supported by a separate budget. This educational opportunity should be available for all children regardless of residential location or financial status of the parents.

Musical Activities. Wherever an educational program is found in any of the above mentioned schools, music activities will also be found. Parents and teachers should be alert for pre-school experiences which will abet the following.

1. Encourage pleasant, satisfying, and meaningful expressions through music, thus leading the child to recognize singing and bodily movement as normal and natural ways of interpreting, understanding, and enriching his daily life.

2. Direct the attention of the child to the sound of music and movement to music in his home and school environment.

3. Encourage creative expression in children but maintain a respect for individual difference of talents and tastes; evaluate the early musical creative efforts with adult understanding.

4. Provide a broad foundation for future musical experiences through listening, singing, and dancing, by using simple melodic and rhythmic instruments.

All pre-school musical activities should be experienced both individually and as a part of a group. These activities should include those which are directed and undirected, voluntary and organized. If the singing habits and musical interests of the mother have been sufficient, the child will participate naturally in all types of musical activities, but if the first contact with music is made in a school environment, sufficient time should be allowed for the very young child to develop an interest in music and a desire to participate. The reader is reminded that the chapters comprising Part I of this Section deal with specific activities which should be considered along with the material which follows.

Singing

As singing is the first and fundamental music activity, its importance is readily understood. It not only stands alone as an activity but has a relationship to all other musical activities. Very small children naturally have light, small speaking voices and their singing voices should be correspondingly light and small with a flute-like quality. Songs for small singers should be short, have rhythmic flow and unity, and be suitable to the age and experience of the child. It is an asset if the songs contain large intervals and regular scale progressions. Selections having a tone repeated several times in succession are helpful for voices having pitch difficulty. All work with conversational singers should be done in connection with a song or a game and done in the spirit of play. It is necessary for the teacher to sing a great deal *for* very young children using a light pleasing voice.

Singing Games

From a physiological viewpoint it may be considered inadvisable to sing and play at the same time, however, the natural outlet of joyousness is to burst into song while playing. It is therefore necessary to keep both of these facts in mind when selecting singing games.

Ideally the trunk of the body should not be moved while singing. This would eliminate such actions as stooping, bending at the waist, jumping, and all violent exercises. No objection can be found to movements of the arms or perhaps walking. If the motions of the game are strenuous, it is well to have one group of children sing while another group plays and then alternate. Many games are so planned that pupils stand still while singing a verse but skip or make suitable motions while the piano or phonograph repeats the tune, the children stopping again when the time comes to sing. Such games as *The Farmer in the Dell* and *In and Out the Windows,* where only a few children are involved in the actions, may be accepted for the joy of all.

The following items should be considered in selecting games for small children whether they be singing games or for purely rhythmic purposes.
1. Informal grouping is desirable.
2. They should be simple in direction and short duration to hold the interest.
3. Many children should have a part.
4. Both quiet and active games should be used.
5. The activity should be suitable to the space available.
6. Participation should require little skill.

Fundamental Rhythms and Mood

Rhythm pulses through the entire body and a small child will sway unconsciously or make some sort of bodily motion whenever he hears music with a marked accent or with a stirring rhythm. One has only to watch little children when a band marches by to see this fact demonstrated. This free and natural rhythmic response to music should not be hampered in the pre-school child but rather responsibility taken for its development.

Little children should have opportunities to express themselves by movement which is based upon listening to accent, rhythmic pattern, or mood. Such activity might be developed by asking the child to name what he wishes to represent such as a bird, falling leaves, snow-flakes, or soldiers, then play several selections on the piano or phonograph and have him choose which one represents what he is. This idea may originate or develop from the free conversation period. For example: if the teacher plays a lullaby and asks what the music says to do, the natural response would be to sit quietly with eyes closed, nod the head, or sway as a cradle. If a march is played, the child would think of action immediately and not repose. A light and airy piece of music would suggest dancing or tripping on tip-toes. It should take very few suggestions to cause the young child to sense or feel the difference between a marching, resting, and a skipping rhythm. Opportunity should be given for recognition of contrast in tempo by having the children listen and then change their movements to interpret a new tempo or rhythmic pattern.

Besides free rhythmic response, many directed responses should be experienced, such as marching, skipping, skating (sliding of feet), slow walking (elephant walk), hopping, flying (moving the arms up and down while running on tip-toe), high stepping horses, etc. The child will learn to feel the music suitable for these bodily movements with only an occasional suggestion from the teacher.

In all rhythmic work it is unadvisable for the teacher to indicate the rhythm audibly in such ways as patting the foot or snapping the fingers. The stimulus for action should come from a pulsation from within and not as a reaction to sounds from without. Rhythmic responses should not be conducted as a drill for when the teacher sets a pattern and the child imitates, he does not grow in self expression but tends to lose initiative.

Rhythm bands which have been discussed in Chapter V are an important part of pre-school rhythmic activity. The material should be simple and the activity should not be stressed to the exclusion of singing, dancing, quiet listening, and creating.

It is important to remember that listening permeates all rhythmic activity and all response to mood expressed in music.

The Teacher. Those in charge of pre-primary children should have training in techniques and materials suitable for use with very young children. It is imperative that the teacher have a desirable singing voice and an ability to play simple accompaniments to all songs as well as selections for rhythmic activities. It is neither desirable nor advisable for the teacher to sing *with* the children at *all* times, nor to play the piano with *all* singing. If judgment is used in this matter, the independence and confidence of the child can be established easily. These two attributes, independence and confidence, are tremendously important.

Evaluation. Any musical activity at this age level should be evaluated in the light of careful planning and preparation made for the activity. The program of activities should be well balanced and show progress from day to day. An increased participation in music activities showing progress and development is an indication of success and a fine test is the frequency with which the child requests activities which involve music. The emotional tone of the group will indicate the group control and will be influenced by the amount of participation of each child.

By pre-primary school attendance a child should have learned to give attention for listening purposes, established social habits such as non-interference with hands and feet, to start and stop with the music, skill and control of bodily movements, willingness to take part and to make suggestions, a repertoire of songs, and contact with instrumental selections.

9 MUSIC IN THE PRIMARY GRADES

The term *Primary Grades* embraces the first, second, and third grade levels of the elementary school. These years of a child's life, representing a possible span from their fifth through eighth years, are formative and of utmost importance educationally. Habits and reaction patterns are being established and certain curiosities and interests are exceedingly strong.

Those teaching music at the primary grade level should be informed as to the general mental and emotional development of this age bracket and should know general teaching techniques which are appropriate.

The Non-Kindergarten School

In the few situations where an organized kindergarten is not a part of the regular school system, the music activities suggested in Chapter VIII "Nursery School, Pre-School, and Kindergarten" will apply to the first grade children. In this case the time consumed for satisfactory accomplishment of the kindergarten attainments will be lessened considerably and the group can progress as they are ready for the next step in the developmental process.

The Five-Fold Program

The five-fold program of music education which was pioneered as an organized procedure in the Cleveland, Ohio, Public Schools,* has been adopted by the Music Educators National Conference and has been utilized by several of the recent basic music text books in series.

For the purpose of sequence and organization of material, it is necessary to indicate levels or grades of accomplishment, however, any good teacher knows that growth and development must begin with a knowledge of the exact status of the children which comprise

*Dr. Russell V. Morgan formulated the "Program for Music Education" when he was serving as Chairman of the MENC Research Council.

the specific group being taught. It is not the intent here to minimize a logical sequence of development but rather to assure the reader that deviations from such an outlined logical sequence are desirable provided the major and ultimate goal is clearly in mind. A complete *Outline of a Program for Music Education* is given on pages 51 and 69.

Singing

Various phases of the singing activity have been discussed in Chapter III and IV. The material in these two chapters is vital for all singing activities in the primary grades.

Accepting the theory that every child should have a place in school music, the importance of the singing activity at the primary level is quickly understood. It includes every child because it has been proven that unless a child is physically defective in his throat or ear, he *can* be taught to sing.

Experiences. The following singing activities should be experienced by all children at the primary level.

(1) Many songs should be taught by rote which are musically interesting and which have texts suitable for the age level. These should be selected to progress from simple four-phrase songs to those which are longer and contain more difficult rhythmic and melodic passages. Furthermore, songs should be chosen with regard to season of the year and utility value at home and school. Standard composers have written songs which are delightful for children to sing. Their use will give acquaintance with these composers and serve as an introduction to music history and literature.

(2) Every 'conversational singer' should have been eliminated by the end of the third grade through the use of songs which will help this wavering voice. Songs with repeated tones certainly should have been used in order to give opportunity for pitch matching. Songs with octave intervals should have helped in realizing a large movement of the voice. (See page 17, Conversational Singers.)

(3) Many singing games will have been played in order to increase the child's desire to participate in musical activities and to aid in the development of freedom of self-expression both vocally and rhythmically.

(4) Through the singing of many lovely and appropriate songs certain talented children may be discovered who should be given an opportunity for additional development in proportion to their interests and abilities. This opportunity may be met in part by the formation of a selected group such as a choir or beginning instrumental instruction. It may be advisable to encourage these talented students to take private music lessons.

44

Attainments. By the end of the third grade, good singing posture should be well established along with an awareness of acceptable singing tone quality. Intonation, enunciation, pronunciation, as well as clearly defined accent, rhythmic flow, and phrasing should have become a part of the child's singing. A large number of songs will have been memorized.

Song books will have been in the hands of the children so that they may visualize some of the songs which have been taught to them by rote. This provides for seeing the contour of the melody, the rhythmic patterns of note combinations, along with a demonstration of the over-all objective in reading-readiness of 'so it sounds,—so it looks'.

Playing

The proper approach to instrumental participation is made through singing and bodily rhythmic activities. The shift from making certain body motions on primary accents to the striking of a drum on these same accents is simple and natural.

Experiences. The following playing activities should have been experienced by all primary children.

(1) In the rhythm orchestra children have the opportunity to become acquainted by ear with some of the elements of music structure and gain an understanding of tempo, mood and interpretation. (See Chapter V.)

(2) Increasingly toy flutes, tonettes, and other pre-orchestral melody instruments are being used as an exploration or introduction to wind instrument playing. This is one of the best ways for identifying those students with natural talent and bent for playing instruments and is recommended for use especially in grade three. The transition from the playing of these exploratory instruments to the playing of a regular instrument in the intermediate grade orchestra is easily made. Pre-orchestra instruments are low in cost and the fact that the whole class may play together is of great advantage. They aid in developing muscular coordination, give a feeling for ensemble, further ear acuteness to pitch and help the note-reading process.

(3) A familiarity with piano keyboard serves as a basis for much instrumental development. The educative values of experience with the piano or other space-frame instruments are generally accepted by all music educators because it calls for collaboration between the eye and the hand as well as the ear and the voice. Beginning piano classes sometimes include outstanding children from grades one and two along with the average third grader. The activities for these

beginning class-piano pupils have been classified under four main headings by a National Committee on *Basic Music Instruction Through Piano Classes* as follows.

"I. Rhythmic games include: (a) swinging the measure, (b) hearing the beats in a measure, (c) guessing the name of a familiar song through the recognition of the rhythm tapped, (d) matching rhythms, where the teacher or a pupil taps a rhythmic phrase and the class repeats it or creates an answering phrase, (e) blackboard games which involve drawing notes, rests, etc., to rhythm, and (f) writing words on the staff by placing notes where the letters are located, for example: cage, beg and cabbage.

II. Ear-training consisting of: (a) distinguishing loud and soft, such as fairies and giants, (b) distinguishing high and low, (c) drawing pitch pictures, (d) listening for the mood of the selection, (e) distinguishing fast and slow, (f) hearing the dominant and tonic chords at the end of phrases.

III. Note games including: (a) approaching notation through story, (b) matching staff notes on piano or keyboard, (c) flash cards containing note patterns, (d) combination of rote and note, (e) phrase-wise reading, and (f) use of blank music notebooks for written work.

IV. Technique which is sufficient for immediate needs should be approached through story and technique games or finger plays, rather than through isolated finger drills.

The criteria for selecting material to be used by beginning class piano pupils are: (a) is it interesting and musical? (b) suitable pitch range for singing, (c) simplicity of finger patterns, (d) repetition of phrases, (e) does it stimulate a desire to read ahead of the assignment? (f) is the development logical? and, (g) general format of the book."*

Attainments. The extent of instrumental contact and attainments at the primary level will depend somewhat upon the equipment available. Through playing of recordings, listening to the radio, or actual instrument demonstration, all children completing the third grade should be able to recognize by sight and to distinguish by ear the distinctive tone quality of the violin, cello, and piano as a minimum.

Rhythms

The primary level is a time of great physical activity. There is really no logical basis for sequencial order for bodily rhythmic activi-

*Music Education Source Book, 1949. Page 88. "Piano Class Curriculum Study Report" Olga E. Prigge, Chairman, MENC. Edited by Hazel B. Morgan.

ties save that of progressive difficulty. Physical coordination and previous rhythmic experience will need to be investigated.

Experiences. The following outline of rhythmic experiences is quite generally accepted.

FIRST YEAR	SECOND YEAR	THIRD YEAR
Singing Games	Singing Games (old and new)	Singing Games
Dramatization	Dramatization (creative)	Dramatization (creative)
Impersonations	Impersonations, Pretending,	Impersonations, Pretending,
Fundamental Movements	Pantomime (creative)	Pantomine (creative)
	Fundamental Movements	Fundamental Movements
	Singing Folk Dances	Singing Folk Dances
		Dance Steps

Attainments. During the primary years, bodily rhythmic activity should have resulted in better rhythmic flow of singing and playing. By the end of the year, the simple rhythms of walking, skipping, etc., will have been developed into dances such as the polka, gavotte, waltz, and schottische. Dramatization will have led to original 'acting out of stories' told by selected program music, and themes of some standard selections from music literature will be recognized by ear.

Listening

The performer as well as the hearer participate in the listening activity. The first step in the presentation of the first rote song involves the child in active listening in order to hear and learn the words and melody. Rhythmic response may be based upon listening to instrumental as well as vocal music. Directed listening gives an acquaintance with music literature and is the beginning of power for musical discrimination which will form in turn a basis for selective judgment. Contact with form in music as well as a knowledge of past and present day composers and artists are furthered through the listening activity.

Experiences. Every activity which involves music has listening as an important part of the activity. The following outline will indicate minimum essentials for primary listening.* The reader will notice that there is considerable inter-relationship.

*"Ohio Elementary Music Guide," Department of Education, State of Ohio, Columbus page 30.

Grade One
1. Quiet listening for:
    (a) Enjoyment of musical beauty and of the mood or story of the selection.
    (b) Music memory and the beginning of a listening repertoire.
2. As a basis of self-expression through:
    (a) Bodily response
    > Clapping, stepping, and swaying
    > Natural rhythms
    > Singing games
    > Marking rhythms with drums, sticks, sand blocks, etc.
    (b) Imaginative response
    > Mimetic play
    (c) Rote singing for appreciation of tone, tune, and mood.

Grades Two and Three
1. Quiet listening for:
    (a) Enjoyment of musical beauty and of the mood or story of the selection.
    (b) Music memory, furthering of a listening repertoire.
    (c) Recognition of simple meter patterns, figurations, phrasing, cadence, etc.
    (d) Recognition of difference in color and feeling of major and minor modes, and of the accompaniment of a song as an harmonic experience.
    (e) Incidental recognition of common types of voices and instruments.
2. As a basis of self-expression through:
    (a) Bodily response
    > (1) Marching, easy dance steps, and simple folk dances.
    > (2) Expression of simple meter patterns, figurations, phrasing and design through bodily movements (Dalcrose), and through original dances.
    > (3) Expression of simple meter patterns, figurations, phrasing and design through rhythm band.
    (b) Imaginative response
    > (1) Simple dramatizations
    > (2) Drawing, painting, modelling, handcrafts, etc.
    > (3) Original stories and poems
    > (4) Original tunes
    (c) Rote singing for finer appreciation of tone, tune, and the mood of the song.
    (d) Music criticism—thinking and talking intelligently about music heard.

Attainments. It is undesirable and practically impossible to state the specific attainments in listening for children who complete the third grade. The important accomplishment should be one of a proper attitude towards listening which is founded upon interest and alertness. The reader should review Chapter VI.

By the end of grade three, due to the listening activity, a ready recognition and differentiation should have been established for the following as a bare minimum in regard to music heard.
1. Whether the music heard is fast or slow
2. Whether the music sounds high or low
3. Whether the music is loud or soft

And further, to be able to make combined observations, for example: if a child decides that the selection is slow moving, he should also decide whether the music is slow and high (or low) and also soft (or loud). Additional related factors should be a natural outcome of active listening.

Creating

Two definite attitudes will need to be established toward creating as an important phase of musical development. These are, (a) an acceptance of the idea that everyone tries to formulate and present that which is new to him, and (b) that there is no real right and wrong to the things created but rather a differentiation between appropriateness and inappropriateness, whether the offering is satisfactory or unsatisfactory. The creative concept will cut across the other four divisions of the primary music program, namely: singing, playing, dancing, and listening.

Experiences. Numerous activities and procedures are to be found in Chapter VII. In all forms of creative work, the teacher must know that it will flourish better under encouragement than censure and that a child deserves approval and recognition for his sincere efforts. Furthermore, the teacher will need to know when to guide and when to leave the child to his own resources. Certainly no uniformity of creative expression should be expected. The emphasis will move gradually from simple and spontaneous expression to a consideration of the results that are produced.

Attainments. It would be a happy situation if every child could complete the primary grades with real assurance within him that he, himslef, can make music, that these musical offerings which he makes spontaneously from his own thinking are acceptable to others for what they are and a source of pleasure and satisfaction to himself.

All reading, whether it be just words or words and music, needs to be preceded by certain experiences which familiarize the eye and acquaint the child with the printed page. The rote singing activity is the fore-runner of note reading, both vocal and instrumental, and occupies an important place in the music reading readiness program.

It would be well for those teaching children to read music to be informed on the techniques used for teaching children to read the vernacular. The proportionate importance of note reading skill in the over-all music education program may be had from the following.

"Music education may be conceived as having five recognized areas, namely: (a) aesthetic experience, (b) emotional development, (c) creative attitudes, (d) social values, and (e) skills and knowledges."*

This listing clearly indicates the relatively small part which skill occupies in the entire picture of education through music. Skill in music may be interpreted to mean technical skill, that is, vocal control which includes muscular and breath, and digital dexterity. But these skills would be quite useless unless they are accompanied by a music reading skill or ability to interpret the symbols of music notation.

Some of the basic concepts for all reading include the following, and the application which can be made to the reading of printed music is very apparent.

1. Preparation. Reading readiness has many phases such as, maturation, muscular control, sufficient background of experiences, etc.

2. Skill. This might be called technique or speed and accuracy.

3. The recognition of symbols and an ability to apply knowledge of their meaning.

4. The audible pronouncement or the vocal element.

Practically all primary schools are equipped with basic music text books to be placed in the hands of children. It should be assumed that these books have been compiled by editors who are well informed as to the proper reading readiness procedures and techniques. The manuals for teachers which accompany these various series indicate quite clearly how the material was intended to be used to achieve an adequate background of reading readiness as well as the initial steps in the actual reading of new music. It should be unnecessary to indicate the importance of a careful study of these

*"Functioning of Fundamental Reading Concepts in Music Education," by Hazel B. Nohavec (Morgan). Sixth Annual Reading Conference Report, Claremont Colleges Library, Claremont, California. 1941, p. 85.

accompanying manuals but many primary teachers fail to study them and so their teaching is ineffective.

Attainments. Attainments at any grade level can only approximate average situations because, in addition to the normal-average child in any class, will be found some children with unusual musical talents, interests, and home backgrounds, as well as a few who seemingly lack both interest and musical ability. This is true in all subjects and at all grade levels so it should not be considered a unique situation for music by music teachers.

A music program for the primary grade level which is well balanced as to variety of activity, which has been presented with a positive approach, will progressively widen the music horizons of children in grades one, two, and three, and develop not only performance techniques, but give an appreciation and understanding of all music. These accomplishments will lead to a further enjoyment of music in all its phases and a natural desire to have further study and contacts with music.

Outline of Music Program—Primary Grades*

1. *Listening*
   a. Enjoyment
   b. Learning by rote
   c. Developing musicality

2. *Singing*
   a. Learning to use voices better
   b. Learning songs
   c. Choir experience
   d. Assembly singing

3. *Motion to Music*
   a. Mimetic play and creative rhythmic activities
   b. Simple eurythmics
   c. Singing games and simple folk dances

4. *Playing an Instrument*
   a. Rhythm and melody instruments
   b. Class piano

5. *Creative Activity*
   a. Rhythmic interpretation
   b. Songs and continuities for units and programs

6. *Introduction to Notation—Eye Training*

*From MENC Publication.

10 MUSIC IN THE INTERMEDIATE GRADES

The fourth, fifth, and sixth grades are designated as upper elementary or intermediate grades. The age bracket for children of these grades extends from nine to eleven years, which means that with few exceptions, the concern would be with immediate pre-adolescent children.

The musical background of pupils entering the intermediate grades will vary according to the program of music teaching which was followed in the preceding grades. Each year should begin with a brief exploratory period which will allow the teacher to discover the level at which the music teaching must be begun. The chief items that will need to be known are:

(1) The extent of previous contact with song literature. It is usually possible to find folk and patriotic songs which are familiar to the entire class. The class may be unified quickly by the teaching of a few songs by rote which are new to the entire class. These songs should be chosen carefully as to word content because it must be remembered that these children are no longer classed as primary children.

(2) The level of reading readiness. If music reading has been introduced in the late primary grades, an exploration of the extent of progress will reveal the stage of transference from rote singing to note reading, and indicate the difficulty of the music reading material to be presented. (See Chapter XI.)

(3) General attitude towards singing. If the interest in singing is inactive or lacking, this will need to be discovered immediately and be stimulated and encouraged.

The intermediate grade teacher will have use for a working knowledge not only of child psychology, but also of adolescent psychology and teaching techniques which will aid in encouraging and guiding the learning process of pre-adolescent children. The items which were indicated for the primary grades in Chapter IX, namely: singing, playing, rhythms, listening, and creating carry over into and progress through grades four, five and six. To this five-fold program is added the development of skill in note reading.

The singing voices in this age bracket will have more stability and the attitude toward all musical activities, especially singing, should be one of naturalness. The interest in singing will depend largely upon the material used, the methods of presentation, and the sincere enthusiasm of the teacher.

Rote Songs. The number of songs taught by rote will be less in these grades than in the primary grades because the children will be able to read many songs, some of which will be worthy of memorization. The rote songs which are presented should be gems of literature and become a part of the child's lasting repertoire.

Songs to Be Read. A basic music book in the hands of each child and access to one or more sets of supplimentary music reading books will provide adequate material for song reading. Further discussion will be found under the heading of "Music Reading" later in this chapter.

The Tune-less Child. Only a very few children will be found in the intermediate grades who can be classed as *conversational singers*. The following suggestions should be followed in the intermediate grades with those who cannot sing a tune correctly in regard to pitch.

(1) Medical Inspection. If preceding teachers have failed to give a child control of his singing voice, the chances are that there may be some physical defect and the advice of the school nurse or physician should be sought. If this defect is plainly visible by a lay person, the child should not be made conspicuous in the group but should be assured that his best is acceptable to both the teacher and the members of the class.

(2) Individual Help. If the child has been unfortunate in having primary teachers who, for lack of time, ability, or appreciation of the importance, have failed to give him the ability to move his voice according to a tune pattern, he should be given special help or drill. (See Chapter IV.) This child should not be singled out during the music class for two very obvious and logical reasons.

  (a) He has reached an age where he is self-conscious of his seeming lack of ability to match his voice with the rest of the class and so tends to withdraw. Any tenseness or embarassment will only hinder his efforts to sing.

  (b) The problem of non-singers should not take an undue proportion of the class time in the intermediate grades in fairness to the other members of the class.

(3) Wing-method of Seating. Much fine development has resulted for physically normal children who reach the intermediate grades but who cannot sing due to lack of experience, by using the 'wing-method'. By this is meant the selecting of a child who has strong

ability and a friendly attitude to take the inexperienced one 'under his wing'. They may sit together or adjacently and help be given from the stronger to the weaker until progress is sufficient to 'fly alone'. This should not be done in a conspicuous or labored manner but rather a natural and friendly assistance.

Part Singing. From the very beginning of the singing experience, one part or unison songs have been used. Various hearing experiences are useful in preparing the ear for part singing. These will have been presented in an incidental fashion, perhaps, but are none the less important.

Experiences for Part Singing Readiness

Ideally these part singing readiness experiences will be introduced when the ability of the child warrants it and in certain instances, when the material lends itself to harmonization.

(1) Accompaniments. Even in the kindergarten, children should hear simple accompaniments played while they sing familiar songs. Alert teachers will have played a simple harmony part while the children sing the tune for the definite purpose of accustoming the ear to hearing two tones sounded simultaneously. Some of the better basic music text books give suggestions for chording which may be played on auto-harp or piano by the teacher or, preferably, by a student. It is to be lamented that more pianos are not readily available for use in the intermediate grades where they would serve a vital purpose in part singing readiness.

(2) Teacher Sings. When a song is well known by the class, the teacher may sing an alto or transposed tenor harmony just as an embellishment. This is one example of where it is proper and advantageous for the teacher to sing both *with* and *for* the children.

(3) Rounds and Descants. It can be argued that the contribution of rounds and descants to part singing preparation may be negligible due to the fact that the major attention is centered upon the tune line rather than upon 'tone against tone'. To put it another way, the importance is placed on *horizontal* music listening instead of *perpendicular* listening. However, three values can be present while singing rounds if the teacher so desires, namely: (a) at a given signal, the tones being sung may be held to enable all to hear the correctness of pitch and beauty of sound, (b) there is pleasure in singing two melodies simultaneously and it can develop self assurance in the individual which is an asset for part singing, and, (c) unified primary accent must be maintained while a descant or round is sung. The tunes *pace* each other instead of *race* each other, which means that the parts must be *in step*.

(4) Chords and Progressions. This may be considered by some as abstract or unrelated drill but even in the light of the aura of ultra-progressive education, repetition with a specific purpose is still one of the important laws of learnings. Skills need some drill or practice whether it be penmanship, vernacular reading, or music reading. If these drills are purposeful, intelligently conducted, and directly related to the material being studied, they will be profitable and pleasant, but they should consume a very small portion of the class time. Many techniques may be used but written notation from the blackboard and oral dictation are the most common.

(a) Examples of two-part written notation from the blackboard. The teacher may write on the blackboard and, giving the correct pitch, asks half of the class to sing "one" or "do".

Then a note a third above is added and this

pitch, "three" or "mi", is sung by the remainder of the class thus calling attention to the appearance and the sound of two tones being sung simultaneously.

This technique may be enlarged as follows. The teacher may write on the blackboard and, giving the initial pitch, ask one half of the room to sing "one - seven - one" or "do - ti - do".

Then writing the other half of the room is asked

to sing "three - four - three" or "mi - fa - mi". If these groups of three notes have been sung correctly they may be sung simultaneously so that what was seen and heard as

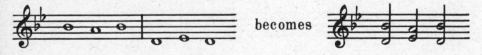 becomes

Combinations of two notes in various keys seen and heard simultaneously will familiarize both the ear and eye with combinations encountered in two-part music reading. Other appropriate two tone combinations suggested are:

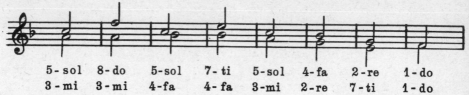

5 - sol	8 - do	5 - sol	7 - ti	5 - sol	4 - fa	2 - re	1 - do
3 - mi	3 - mi	4 - fa	4 - fa	3 - mi	2 - re	7 - ti	1 - do

By using different keys and note combinations, the eye and ear will be aided in the process of 'so it looks, so it sounds'.

(b) Examples of three-part written notation from the blackboard.

The teacher may write  on the blackboard, and

giving the correct starting pitch, ask one third of the room to sing "one - seven - one" or "do - ti - do"

Then writing  another third of the room is

asked to sing "three - four - three" or "mi - fa - mi".

Then 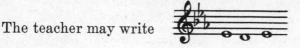 may be written on the black-

board and the remaining third of the room asked to sing "five - five - five" or "sol - sol - sol". The next logical step is to have the tone groups sung simultaneously so that what was heard as

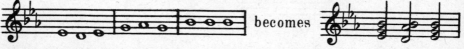 becomes

The use of three notes in combination in different keys seen and heard simultaneously will further develop a consciousness of ear and eye relationship. Other three-tone combinations suggested are:

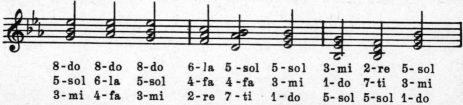

8 - do	8 - do	8 - do	6 - la	5 - sol	5 - sol	3 - mi	2 - re	5 - sol
5 - sol	6 - la	5 - sol	4 - fa	4 - fa	3 - mi	1 - do	7 - ti	3 - mi
3 - mi	4 - fa	3 - mi	2 - re	7 - ti	1 - do	5 - sol	5 - sol	1 - do

(c) Examples of oral dictation. Syllables, numbers, or letters may be used for oral dictation. Oral dictation may be given by dictating one tone at a time, for example: the teacher may give the key pitch and say, "one" or "do", indicating that section of the class which is to sing it; then she may say "three" or "mi" and the rest of the room sings this pitch while the "one" or "do" is being held. Oral dictation may be given by dictating several tones at a time, for example: the teacher may establish the starting tones as indicated in the previous sentence and then dictate "one - seven - one" or "do - ti - do" indicating the section of the class singing the initial tone of "one" or "do", and say "three - four - three" or "mi - fa - mi" indicating the section singing the initial tone of "three" or "mi". At a signal of the teacher's hand, the students sing the three tones dictated for their section.

The above examples have been given for two parts only but the chords and progressions should be extended to include three or even four parts as well as more than three tones in the sequence dictated. It should be remembered that drill of this type is only proper when it serves an immediate purpose and *should not be used in abstraction when it can be related to the songs being studied.*

Introduction of Two-Part Singing

All that is necessary to sing music in two parts is to divide the room through the center, front to back, and have each side take the beginning tone of their respective parts and proceed to read the line of notes assigned to them. It is a mistaken idea to have half of the room listen while one side practices and, when the parts are mastered separately, sing them at the same time. This is two-part singing but only one-part reading. If after attempting to read the song as two parts simultaneously and failing in the same place several times, it may be advisable to stop and work on that specific note group, each part separately. If this is necessary, be sure to practice the lower part first, because it seems to be more difficult for children to sing a lower harmony after hearing the tune.

Voices do not require testing in grade five and material usually used for beginning two-part singing is written in the range of two sopranos. Therefore, it is desirable to alternate sides of the room, not within the song but on every other song. For example, if the left-hand side of the room sings the lower part of the new song today; tomorrow, if a new two-part song is studied, the left-hand side of the room will sing the upper part. The problem is not whether the children can sing the upper and lower part of the same song, but whether they can carry an upper or lower harmony. This permits the use of a much larger number of songs and is advisable from many angles.

An exceptionally low voice may be found occasionally in grade five. This child should be placed in the center row of the room and told that he may sing with whichever division has the lower notes. To insure good two-part singing, the children who prove that they can carry the lower part well should be distributed so that there will be leaders and balance whichever way the assignment of parts is made. Even though the class can sing two-part songs well, some songs in unison should be used.

Introduction of Three-Part Singing

It is interesting to note that physical maturation, musical interest and, it is hoped, musical ability, ripen or converge at about the sixth grade level so that the singing of three-part songs becomes logical and natural. While pupils were in grade five, their voices have had experience with singing both an upper and lower harmony which constitutes one of the readinesses for three-part material. Three-part songs are written for soprano, second-soprano, and alto voices and necessitate the testing of voices and the assignment to sing definite parts. This is really the outstanding difference between the music work of grades five and six.

Voice Testing. It is an erroneous idea to think that the testing of voices is difficult, though this may be true if the teacher is without proper training. Voice testing requires exactness of pitch and quality, a knowledge of child voice, and a very definite understanding of the thing to be accomplished. If the one doing the testing is in doubt about the exact sound of the alto or soprano quality, it is well to listen to recordings of voices so classified. The quality once recognized is quite easily retained.

The need for testing is not that the voices are changing, (often confused with the changing of a boy's voice into a man's voice) but on account of the voices becoming more stable and the ranges becoming more fixed. As he grows older, the child's tones become more established and divide themselves into good tones which should be used, and bad tones which should not be used. Children of this age are subject to physical changes which tend toward temporary or perhaps a permanent shifting of the child's voice register. It is therefore necessary to test voices often. Neither the teacher nor the pupil should look upon voice testing as an ordeal but rather something as simple as trying on a shoe to see if it will fit. The voice is tested to see if the *good* tones will fit certain singing parts.

The teacher's judgment will tell whether psychologically it is wise to ask a child to stand alone and have his voice tested. Some children are easily embarrassed and shy, the test under these circumstances would be a failure. It may be well to have two pupils standing, one singing and the other ready to sing; or to have a whole row of chil-

58

dren stand at one time, singing the test together with the teacher listening to them individually. To test properly, each voice must be listened to separately. The two things to be decided upon are range and quality. It is necessary to know how far a child can reach with his voice (range), but the deciding factor must be how his voice sounds (quality). That portion of the range which has good quality indicates the singing part to which the voice should be assigned.

General Methods of Voice Testing Procedure

Four simple exercises serve quite satisfactorily to locate all unchanged voices on the proper part. The voices of some pupils can be classified after the instructor has heard only one exercise sung. Other voices may demand the use of all exercises.

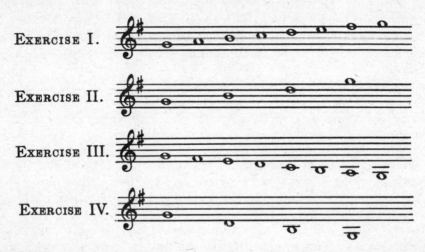

Syllable names, numbers, or the neutral syllable "loo", may be used for singing the test. It is well to have the child take a breath at the end of each exercise because this shows his breath control and gives the teacher an opportunity to listen and check his accuracy of pitch. If a child flats in the exercise, he is trying to reach too high, if he sharps, he is reaching too low.

Many children seem to feel that when they are once classified as a soprano or alto that they will always belong to that part. In some instances perhaps they will, but many boys will have the experience of singing all parts, caused by their voices gradually dropping until they are at last singing bass. Because the first testing is done in grade six, and because frequently it is necessary to re-test and make shifts in parts, it often has been found advisable to defer naming the voice until the junior high school is reached. The terms first or high, second or middle, and third or low may be used instead of first soprano, second soprano, and alto.

(1) The First or High Part. The voices that are classified as belonging to the first or high part must be able to sing up to a high "G" (first space above the staff) with a clear, light, brilliant quality, with no tightening of the throat nor scowling of the face. If there is much doubt about either the quality or range, it is well to place them on the second or middle part until one is certain.

RANGE OF THE FIRST OR HIGH PART

(2) The Third or Low Part. Likewise, the voices that are to be classified as belonging to the third or low part must be able to sing down to a low "G" (third space below the staff) with a solid, substantial, open tone quality. The tone of those assigned to sing the third part should broaden as it descends in pitch. Any child about whose voice the director is in doubt, should be re-tested for the second part.

RANGE OF THE THIRD OR LOW PART

(3) The Second or Middle Part. It would seem that all pupils who cannot qualify as a first or a third are left for the second part. Such is not the case. The tone quality of the second is neither extremely full nor extremely light, and the range lies between "C" (first line below the staff) or "B♭" (second space below the staff) and "E" (fourth space). The group singing the middle part will need to be further divided into high-seconds and low-seconds. Those voices classified as high-seconds have a soprano quality but have the range of the second part, that is, limited in the upper range. Those voices that possess an alto quality but have the range of the seconds are classified as low-seconds. The low-seconds are limited in their lower range. This division of those singing the second part is necessary on account of the two-part singing. When singing in two parts, the high-seconds sing with the firsts and the low-seconds sing with the thirds.

RANGE OF THE SECOND OR MIDDLE PART

Seating for Three-Part Singing

In the fifth grade the children have become accustomed to two-part singing and making their voices harmonize with one other part. In order that this problem may be continued and not made more difficult, it is well to seat the pupils singing the highest part in the center of the room, with the thirds on one side and the seconds on the other.

Thirds	Firsts	High Seconds	Low Seconds
	Front of Room		

The real test of sixth grade singing comes in the reading of notes to new material in three parts. The key tone of the selection should be sounded and the beginning tone of the respective groups given. The parts should then be read simultaneously. It may be necessary to go back over some particular group of notes after the first trial, but it is well to assume that the children are going to read the selection as three parts. Frequently, groups read one part at a time, then sing them all three together and imagine that they are really doing three-part reading. In case it becomes necessary to take any of the parts alone, it is well to begin with the lowest part, then take the middle part, and lastly, the highest part, or tune. This is done for the same reason as stated in the discussion of two-part singing.

Lesson Order of Procedure

In all grades, the singing lesson should begin with a familiar song which the children have previously memorized. This should be followed by the new work or "kernel" of the lesson. The singing period should close with a song from memory which all enjoy singing.

PLAYING

The program of instrumental music activities in the intermediate grades should be planned so as to accomplish the following.

(1) To give a background of information concerning the more important standard musical instruments.

(2) To afford opportunity for encouragement of the study of a selected instrument.

(3) To enrich, integrate, and socialize the over-all music program by participation in ensembles which will result in enjoyment and general musical progress.

Experiences. The playing of instruments at this grade level should be considered from two points of view, namely: that which involves the entire class as a unit, and that which involves selected students. The playing experiences indicated for the primary grades such as the rhythm orchestra may be continued, not as a repetition but as an experience progressing in difficulty and meaningful development.

Piano Class

Piano classes should be begun, or extended if they have been organized previously in grade three. Some larger cities conduct piano classes on a grade-room basis for at least one semester or one school term. This is done to give a uniform piano experience background in grade four and serves as a basis for future selection. It is advisable to recommend private piano instruction for students who show sufficient progress and outstanding talent, but it is unwise to recommend specific private music teachers.

String Instrument Classes

Where it is not possible to maintain separate classes for each of the string instruments, a combined string class often called a 'string orchestra class', is desirable. This would include violin, viola, 'cello, and string bass. The string bass should be included only if a small size instrument is available. Some music educators prefer to start all members of the string class on the violin and 'cello and then transfer selected students to the viola and string bass when the student enters junior high school. In many schools it may be advisable to stress only violin class lessons.

Students who desire to enroll in string classes will need to have a left hand which can spread to play the intervals on all four strings and his right arm will need to be sufficiently long to draw the bow at the correct angle. Small children do very well using half or three-quarter size instruments but the bow used by these little folk should be of proper length and weight. Good muscular coordination as well as a fine sense of pitch and rhythm is essential.

Attainments. The minimum attainment for string class instruction at the close of the sixth grade would include, (a) automatic correct playing position, (b) ability to tune instrument, (c) good tone production, (d) mastery of common bowings for phrasing, rhythm, attack, and release, (e) a knowledge of first position finger combinations for violin and viola players, additional 'cello and string bass positions for music of similar difficulty,* (f) general understanding of technique for shifting positions, (g) ability to use third and fifth positions in simple music, (h) an extension of knowledge of music theory and literature for their instrument, and (i) ability to play alone and in ensemble.

Wind Instrument Classes

If the number enrolled is sufficient, it is advantageous to have one class for brass instruments and another class for woodwind instruments, but all can be handled in a single class quite successfully. Due to the large number of different instruments which may be involved in a general wind instrument class, stress should be given to the formation of small ensembles such as trios, quartets, etc., within the class membership.

It is normally considered advantageous for those who desire to play brass instruments to have even upper and lower teeth with no gaps. Even lower teeth are an asset for single reed players, but those with irregular upper and lower teeth seem to have little difficulty with the oboe and bassoon, double reed instruments. Successful flute playing requires even lower teeth and sufficient arm length to hold the flute in normal playing position with the fingers approaching the keys at right angles. A wide finger spread in both hands is helpful for all woodwind players in order to reach and cover the keys properly. The right arm of a slide trombone player should be sufficiently long to reach the seventh position.

Attainments. The items which may be regarded as minimum attainment after one term of wind instrument class attendance are, (a) correct playing position, (b) ability to adjust instrument for playing in tune, (c) beautiful and correct tone production, (d) proper breath control, (e) mastery of technique for phrasing, attack and release, (f) working knowledge of the mechanics of the instrument; valve and slide combinations for brass instruments, keys and pads for woodwind instruments, (g) knowledge of finger combinations and appropriate substitutions, (h) extension of knowledge of theory

*Some music educators feel it is inadvisable to use violas or string basses at the intermediate grade level.

with emphasis on tonic, sub-dominant and dominant chords, and (i) acquaintance with solo and ensemble literature.

Elementary School Orchestra and Band

The elementary school orchestra and band will draw most players from the intermediate grades, but proficient players from the primary grades, if housed in the same building, should be eligible for membership. These organizations should not be open to rank beginners but should be an activity for members who have studied their instruments previously and have the ability to play parts in the ensemble.

The orchestra is favored over the band at this grade level because it provides an opportunity for both string and woodwind players. Large elementary schools should have both a band and an orchestra. It has been found that if strings are stressed in these grades, a balanced program of instrumental music can be achieved in the junior and senior high school.

While a balanced instrumentation is very desirable, this lack should not deter the organization of an 'assemblage of players' which can be dignified by the use of the name 'band' or 'orchestra'. Certain substitutions may serve a real purpose and gradually the desired instrumentation may be achieved.

SUGGESTED INSTRUMENTATION FOR
ELEMENTARY SCHOOL ORCHESTRAS

4-6 first violins	1-2 flutes	1-2 tubas
4-6 second violins	2-4 clarinets	1-2 drums
4-6 third violins	2-3 cornets	1-2 pianos
4-6 'cellos	1-2 trombones	1-2 saxophones

SUGGESTED INSTRUMENTATION FOR
ELEMENTARY SCHOOL BANDS

2-4 flutes	4-6 cornets	1 bass drum
6-12 clarinets	2-3 trombones	1-2 snare drums
1-2 E flat saxophones	2-4 horns (or mellophones)	1 cymbals
1-2 tenor saxophones	2-3 tubas	

Attainments. Membership in the elementary school orchestra or band should give: (a) added incentive for individual practice, (b) acquaintance with all instruments, (c) ability to adjust the playing tone for solo, choir, or full ensemble, (d) wider acquaintance with music literature, (e) practice in following a director, and (f) additional basic skill which will lead to participation in more advanced organizations.

Small Instrumental Ensembles

A group of from three to eight players, each one of whom plays a separate and distinct part, is called an ensemble. When members of an orchestra or band are also members of ensembles, the playing of the larger group is enhanced greatly.

Many general purposes may be served beyond the specific benefit to the players, for example: for programs when a larger group would be unwieldly or undesirable, and it solves the problem of over-balance when there is a surplus of players for larger groups.

A recently published instrumental series has provided music so that any or all instruments present in a classroom can play with selected songs, read and sung by the entire class. This is an ideal arrangement and is very much in keeping with the concept of an integrated music program.

RHYTHMIC ACTIVITIES—DANCING

If the rhythmic activities in the primary grades have been varied and adequate, there will have taken place a gradual transition from outward bodily movements to an inner response to rhythm. This should be present and discernable in intermediate grade children by their ability to identify patterns or figurations as well as contrasts or repetitions in music notation whether vocal or instrumental. If this has not been accomplished, it will be necessary for fourth grade children to experience some of the elementary but fundamental rhythmic activities.

Folk songs and dances are a spontaneous expression of the feeling and thinking of the people of the country where they originated. Due to the nature of their origin and development, they are ideal material for intermediate grade use and give a general understanding which can be achieved in no other way. All basic music texts include much folk material and directions for their use may be found in the corresponding teacher's manuals.

Attainments. Rhythmic patterns encountered in music to be read should be quickly recognized by eye and be played or sung correctly. Clapping of rhythmic patterns or audible counting should have served its purpose and its use reduced to a minimum by the end of grade six.

The following standard types of folk dances in addition to marching, running, and skipping, should be familiar to all children before entering the junior high school: (1) waltz, (2) polka, (3) mazurka, (4) minuet, (5) gavotte, (6) polonaise, (7) American square dance.

LISTENING

As a child progresses through the grades it becomes increasingly important to establish the habit of quiet listening which in reality is a substitution of mental activity for physical activity. It cannot be emphasized too often that listening takes place in some form and to some degree in every music lesson. It is the duty of the teacher to be aware of this, making the most of every opportunity which presents itself.

Experiences. The areas to be stressed in the intermediate grades are chiefly for the purposes of enjoyment, rote learning, furtherance of musicality, and preparation for concert attendance. The following outline* will indicate minimum essentials for listening activities at these grade levels.

Grades IV, V, and VI
1. Quiet listening for:
    - (a) Enjoyment of musical beauty and mood or story of the selection.
    - (b) Music memory and the enrichment of listening repertoire.
    - (c) Recognition of meter and figuration patterns, phrasing, melodic motifs, etc.
    - (d) Recognition of difference in color and feeling of major and minor modes and of diatonic and chromatic progressions, and recognition of simple chords, I, IV, and V.
    - (e) Recognition and appreciation of tone color of instruments.
    - (f) Recognition of dance types and simple musical forms.
    - (g) Knowledge of composers through their music and from brief biographical sketches.
    - (h) Appreciation of the background of music through glimpses of history, literautre, and the sister arts.
2. As a basis for self-expression through:
    - (a) Bodily response
        - (1) Expression of meter and figuration patterns, phrasing and design through bodily movement.
        - (2) Interpretation by actual dancing of folk and classic dances which have been studied as dance types in listening lessons.
    - (b) Imaginative response
        - (1) Dramatizations, puppet and shadow plays.

*"Ohio Elementary Music Guide," Department of Education, State of Ohio, Columbus. page 31.

(2) Drawing, painting, modelling, handcraft, etc.
(3) Original stories and poems.
(4) Original tunes and harmonies.
(5) Notebooks, bulletins, displays, etc.
(c) Rote singing as an aid to ear training and richer song repertoire.
(d) Music criticism; learning to think, talk, and write intelligently about music heard; an awareness of newspaper and magazine reports of concerts.

Concerts

Concerts given for children are an integral part of the listening program and includes attendance at actual concerts as well as concerts on recordings, radio, and television. Two extreme examples of concert attendance will serve as an indication of the wide spread possibilities of this activity.*

I. The Small Isolated School

In a town whose population was under five hundred, a wide-awake teacher announced a series of three "Symphony Concerts". She was in charge of a room of forty-seven children and they were in grades four, five, and six.

Pictures of the Boston Symphony Orchestra were displayed in the room. The students became familiar with where the various instruments were seated. The director was discussed until the students felt he was almost a personal friend. Concert deportment was outlined as the result of class discussion so that when they were in a city and attended a symphony concert they would know just how concert-goers act. The program consisted of the *"First Movement of the Fifth Symphony"* by Beethoven, *"The Old Refrain"* played by Fritz Kreisler, and *"Invitation to the Waltz"* by Weber, which were selected largely because they were offered from the library of the lady where the teacher boarded.

After recess, the children came into the room which had been arranged as suitable as possible for the occasion. The atmosphere of a 'special event' was present.

The recordings were played and the children applauded at the proper time and in the proper way. These children had a rich musical experience which was truly educative—all because this teacher was not willing to say that the distances to the cities having orchestras are too great to permit transportation of either the stu-

*Music Education Source Book, edited by Hazel Nohavec Morgan. Music Educators National Conference, Chicago, 1947. Page 138-9. This is original material written by the editor H.N.M.

dents or the performers, so therefore, nothing could be done about it. She was alert to the importance of the situation and was a *real* music teacher.

II. THE LARGE METROPOLITAN SCHOOL SYSTEM

For the past twenty-five years in a large city which is the home of a famous symphony orchestra, children's concerts have been a regular and accepted thing. The School Board has a continuing contract for the School Symphony Series. Instructions and information are not only distributed in bulletin form and by personal visits from the various supervisors, but by radio-casts from the school's own radio station. The programs are arranged by a school board employed music education consultant.

The programs are one hour in length with no intermission. Pre-arranged seating simplifies the entrance and exit of the audience and provides for rotation of the most desirable locations. Each school group is accompanied by a teacher—the only adults present.

Each fourth-grade child may attend one concert, but children above the fourth may attend two concerts each school year. Thus, a child could attend a maximum of seventeen symphony concerts as he progressed from grade four to graduation. The following schedule was followed for a recent school term.

GRADE	NUMBER OF CONCERTS	TOTAL ATTENDANCE
4	3	8,725
5 and 6	10	26,492
7 to 12	8	20,678

This entire school system (students, faculty, and administrators) long have taken for granted the educational values of the concert attendance experience.

Attainments. Progress should be noted in sustained interest in all music as well as ever-increasing discrimination. An important achievement should be a proper attitude towards listening which is based upon increased information and enjoyment. The reader should review Chapter VI.

CREATING

Creative work at any and all grade levels should be directed toward serving the purposes of real education for the child. The dominant attitude of the teacher should be one of encouragement and guidance rather than domination and imposition, permissiveness rather than requirement, with each child working at his own pace according to his native ability. When this teacher attitude is present, an atmosphere conducive to creativeness also will be present in the room.

Experiences. The various items which are indicated in Chapter VII are appropriate for all grade levels and will vary according to the previous experiences of the children. However, each type of activity should broaden and increase in quality as the children mature.

Attainments. The exploratory attitude which was started in the primary grades will lead to the writing of symbols of notation in the intermediate grades. Each child should have developed a respect for the creative efforts of others, especially those of his own age bracket, and coupled with this, a knowledge that his own offerings are acceptable provided he has used his entire resources with discrimination.

Outline of Music Program—Intermediate Grades*

1. *Listening*
   a. Enjoyment
   b. Learning by rote
   c. Developing musicality
   d. Concert preparation

2. *Singing*
   a. Voice development
   b. Song studies
   c. Choir experiences
   d. Assembly singing

3. *Motion to Music*
   a. Eurythmics
   b. Dancing
   c. Dramatization

4. *Playing an Instrument*
   a. Instrumental classes
   b. Small ensembles
   c. Orchestras

5. *Creative Activity*
   a. Performance
   b. Composition

6. *Music Reading*

MUSIC READING

A program for the development of music reading skill needs careful planning and organization in order not to assume undue emphasis in the over-all music program. Because it is tremendously important, because many intermediate grade teachers are uncertain of how to proceed, and because its presentation involves specific attitudes, techniques, etc., Chapter XI has been devoted entirely to this subject.

*From MENC Publication.

MUSIC READING

Two basic facts have been demonstrated beyond refutation and so should be accepted by teachers, pupils, and parents, namely: (a) that music reading is a skill, and (b) that this skill should not be difficult to acquire. It is the lack of knowing how to present music reading and the use of unsuitable materials which make some teachers regard this activity as difficult. In turn, these teachers give their impression of difficultness to the pupils and so erect a barrier which is truly a problem to surmount.

It is important to have in mind before progressing further in this chapter that skill in music reading should be taught in relation to the music at hand and developed as a necessity to furtherance of continuous musical growth.

In the primary grades children were taught songs by rote and observed the music while singing them. Their attention was called to the up-movement and the down-movement of notes on the staff, and was directed to the difference in the appearance of notes and rests. They have experienced bodily rhythms both fast and slow, and recognized the appearance of music which is fast and slow. They have identified by ear and by eye phrases which are like and unlike. When these things have been an integral part of all musical experiences they make a proper background for music reading. The primary grades should be regarded as filled with exploratory experiences and the intermediate grades as an associative period where previous learnings are combined to afford new or extended experiences.

Minimum Tone Combination Recognition

By methods of observation, a ready recognition of notes in combination in songs learned by rote, has been established. The following note combinations usually are considered as a minimum background for beginning note reading but it is not intended that they be presented in isolation from the song or in abstraction. The order of presentation will depend upon their occurance in the song material being read.

(1) Arpeggios and triads ascending and descending.

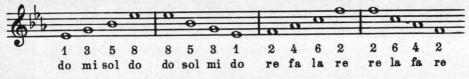

1 3 5 8   8 5 3 1   2 4 6 2   2 6 4 2
do mi sol do   do sol mi do   re fa la re   re la fa re

EXAMPLES OF ARPEGGIOS

Many additional tone groups may be developed from the basis of the arpeggio. The elimination of the upper or lower tone from an arpeggio yields a triad. These should be visualized in several keys.

1 3 5   5 3 1   8 5 3   3 5 8
do mi sol   sol mi do   do sol mi   mi sol do

1 3 5   5 3 1   8 5 3   3 5 8
do mi sol   sol mi do   do sol mi   mi sol do

EXAMPLES OF TRIADS

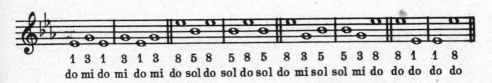

1 3 1   3 1 3   8 5 8   5 8 5   8 3 5   5 3 8   8 1   1 8
do mi do mi do mi do sol do sol do sol do mi sol sol mi do do do do do

EXAMPLES OF ADDITIONAL TONE GROUPS

(2) Three and four tone diatonic combinations ascending and descending.

1 2 3   2 3 4   3 4 5   4 5 6   5 6 7   6 7 8
do re mi   re mi fa   mi fa sol   fa sol la   sol la ti   la ti do

8 7 6   7 6 5   6 5 4   5 4 3   4 3 2   3 2 1
do ti la   ti la sol   la sol fa   sol fa mi   fa mi re   mi re do

EXAMPLES OF THREE-TONE GROUPS ASCENDING AND DESCENDING

1 2 3 4   2 3 4 5   3 4 5 6   4 5 6 7   5 6 7 8

do re mi fa re mi fa sol mi fa sol la fa sol la ti sol la ti do

8 7 6 5   7 6 5 4   6 5 4 3   5 4 3 2   4 3 2 1

do ti la sol ti la sol fa la sol fa mi sol fa mi re fa mi re do

EXAMPLES OF FOUR-TONE GROUPS ASCENDING AND DESCENDING

(3) Neighboring Tones above and below.

1 2 1 1 7 1 2 3 2 2 1 2 3 4 3 3 2 3 4 5 4 etc.

do re do do ti do re mi re re do re mi fa mi mi re mi fa sol fa

EXAMPLES OF NEIGHBORING TONE GROUPS

(4) Repeated Tones. This is entirely a matter of seeing that the note does not move, that it 'sits in the same place' and therefore the voice does not move.

The following analysis of *"Row, Row, Row Your Boat"* illustrates the use of certain tone groups.

Repeated tones   Neighboring tones

3 tone dictonic ascending   3 tone dictonic ascending

Repeated tones Repeated tones Repeated tones Repeated tones 5 tone dictonic descending

Arpeggio

First Sight Songs

Equipped with a working knowledge and recognition of tone groups by syllable or number combinations, the child is ready to 'read to learn'. The first sight songs should include no notes of

72

less than one full beat and no chromatics. The songs should be chosen which consist largely of tone groups with which the child is already familiar by previous observation. Suppose this is the new song to be read:

A   pret - ty   bird   sat   in   a   tree

It   sang   a   song   for   you   and   me.

The teacher might ask the children to find the notes that say what she sings.

Teacher sings:

Mi   do   re   mi
or, 3   1   2   3

The children put their fingers around the group of notes to show it in their books. One child is asked to sing the words and he responds by singing

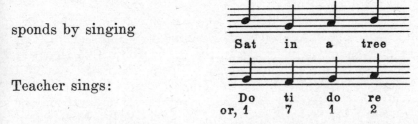

Sat   in   a   tree

Teacher sings:

Do   ti   do   re
or, 1   7   1   2

The children find the notes and one child responds or the class may sing,

It   sang   a   song

Teacher sings:

Sol   do   mi   sol
or, 5   1   3   5

The children respond after finding the notes in their books.

A   pret - ty   bird

Teacher sings:

Fa mi re do
or, 4 3 2 1

Children sing:

For you and me

The motives or tone groups may now be joined and the syllable or number names sung. If the teacher so desires, the tune may be sung using the neutral syllable "loo" after the syllables or numbers have been sung correctly. This may help to emphasize the tune line, however, it may not be necessary with all classes or all songs. The words may be read in the rhythm of the song and the children are now ready to sing the words with the new tune. It should be noted that the above procedure is suggestive and should be adjusted to the specific teaching and learning situation at the discretion of the teacher.

While the studying is going on, it is advantageous for the childrens' music book to be flat on their desks so that they may use both hands if necessary to designate the tone group when it is found. After the practice or study of the song is completed, the music books may be held up with the 'heel' of the book resting on the desk.

It may be necessary for the teacher to chart on the board the more difficult tone groups encountered in new material so that the children may see the movement of the notes in the group for which they are looking. In some of the simpler songs, perhaps the child can find and sing groups with which he is familiar, with no help from the teacher apart from obtaining the proper pitch. If an unusual or totally unfamiliar group appears in the new song, it is proper to treat it just as unfamiliar words in stories, that is, the teacher pronounces it (sings it) for the class.

The children will enjoy singing repeatedly the songs which they read and should be encouraged to memorize those which make a special appeal.

It should be emphasized here that all so-called routines of procedure are simply a means to an end, and that end is new words and music correctly sung at sight. Any step in any procedure which is found unnecessary in reaching the desired goal with certain groups or with certain material, should be eliminated. There are several methods for the presentation of new song material to be read at sight but the preceding technique is quite universally used and readily lends itself to various adaptations.

Chromatics are not difficult to sing because the voice pattern has already been established. They should be presented as something which is easy to sing but which add considerable beauty to the song in which they occur. It is advisable to use the simple chromatic of ♯ 4 and ♭ 7 for chromatic introduction.

(1) Example of ♯ 4   **Sol fi sol**   Voice pattern   **Do ti do**

This pattern should be approached from above and the voice moves as it does in singing do-ti-do, or 8-7-8.

(2) Example of ♭ 7   **La te la**   Voice pattern   **Mi fa mi**

This pattern should be approached from below and the voice moves as it does in singing mi-fa-mi, or 3-4-3.

The presentation of all other sharp chromatics can be developed from the ♯ 4 pattern, and the other flat chromatics can be developed from the ♭ 7 pattern. It should be remembered that chromatics are best presented when they are encountered in new singing material and not as an abstract problem.

Some Simple Rules. The following rules and diagram are for the *information of the inexperienced teacher* who needs to introduce chromatics to her class.

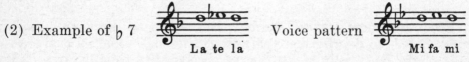

♯ or ♮♭		♭ or ♮♯	
Do			Do
Ti			Ti
La	Li	Te	La
Sol	Si	Le	Sol
Fa	Fi	Se	Fa
Mi			Mi
Re	Ri	Me	Re
Do	Di	Ra	Do

1. To find the syllable name of a note preceded by a sharp, retain the first letter and add the vowel "i" which is pronounced as long "e".

2. To find the syllable name of a note preceded by a flat, retain

the first letter and add the vowel "e" which is pronounced as long "a". There is one exception in the second tone of the scale, when re is preceded by a flat, its name becomes ra, pronounced "rah".

3. A natural which cancels a sharp should be considered as a flat and the rule for flat names apply.

4. A natural which cancels a flat should be considered as a sharp and the rule for sharp names apply.

Development of Rhythmic Patterns

If a feeling for various rhythmic patterns has been established by activities in the primary grades, the patterns found within new songs being studied can be identified and readily utilized. If rhythmic experience has been inadequate or lacking, the following material may be helpful.

Rhythmic Flow of the Words. The words to the song usually hold the key to the rhythmic patterns of the music and an oral scansion of the poem may be all that is necessary to establish the flow.

Abstract Presentation. This heading is included largely for the information of the teacher who, of course, will adapt the presentation to the need of the class being taught and the difficulty of the material being read.

Almost all rhythmic patterns can be classified into three groups for the purpose of abstract presentation and counting.

(1) Notes of one beat or more. These involve quarter notes when the lower time signature figure is 4; eight notes when the lower time signature figure is 8; and half notes when the lower time signature figure is 2.

(2) Equally divided beats. These involve eighth notes when the lower time signature figure is 4; sixteenth notes when the lower time signature figure is 8; and quarter notes when the lower time signature figure is 2.

The use of large up and down motions of the arm are suggested for the development of a rhythmic feeling for divided beat with intermediate children who lack it. One successful way in which the up beat may have an exact terminus is to hold the left hand, palm down about twenty to twenty-four inches above the right thigh when sitting, and to use the right hand to strike the thigh on count one and the back of the right hand contact the left palm on the "and" or the beginning of the last half of the beat.

(3) Unequally Divided Beats. This includes triplets and various rhythmic patterns when the lower time signature figure is 4 or 8.

EXAMPLES OF SOME MEASURES USING NOTES OF ONE OR MORE BEATS

EXAMPLES OF SOME MEASURES USING AN EQUALLY DIVIDED BEAT

EXAMPLES OF SOME MEASURES USING UNEQUALLY DIVIDED BEATS

It is suggested that in $\frac{6}{8}$, $\frac{9}{8}$, and $\frac{12}{8}$ time signatures, the entire count be in numbers as follows with the stress for the primary and secondary accent being given with the voice.

It should be remembered that counting and beating time by either the pupils or the teacher should be used sparingly and only when it is necessary to aid the inner feeling of the pulsation of the music. And further, that the over-all rhythmic flow of the phrase is the real goal in music reading.

(4) Rhythm drill for a specific song. As in all other teaching, specific drills should be used only in aiding the problem at hand. For example, the song, *"Row, Row, Row Your Boat"*, on page 72 has the following measure patterns, which could be isolated and practiced if rhythmic difficulty was encountered.

Song Analysis

In preceding grades the pupils have learned the letter names of the lines and spaces, key letters, the location of the tonic (do or 1), of the key, the meaning of the time signature, and numerous bits of other information as incidentals to songs sung and read. Without much discussion or assistance, the child in the upper intermediate grades should be able to give the following information about this song and understand the meaning.

I know a fair - y Prin - cess.

This song is written in the key of E flat because it has three flats in the signature. 'Do or 1' is found in the fourth space and on the first line of the staff. The time signature is three-quarter, which indicates that there are three counts to a measure and a quarter note receives one count. We begin to sing on the third count of the measure, the name of the first note for the lower part is 'fa or 4', and the first note for the upper part is 'sol or 5'. *Any other form of analysis is just as acceptable provided the needed information is given.*

The details included in this chapter are given in the nature of suggested technical helps. Any technique should be adapted by the teacher to serve the specific purpose in the best fashion. To re-emphasize the simplicity of the music reading process, it should be born in mind that notes can only indicate the movement of the voice in three directions. They either indicate an upward movement of the voice, a downward movement of the voice, or indicate that the voice is not moved at all. The notes used for writing music have only three variations: they may either be open or solid, with or without a stem, and with or without flags. These variations, of course, indicate time duration. Even after letter names are given to lines and spaces of the staff, only seven are used in comparison with the twenty-six in our alphabet!

Music reading ability travels on plateaus, like any other kind of reading. One learns to identify, and then reads for speed and under-standing. An occasional term or symbol will need to be learned as it is encountered in more difficult or advanced notation. This may be regarded as similar to the proper use of the dictionary when reading a story.

Having acquired music reading ability, a student has an avenue for enrichment and enjoyment which will be his as long as he lives; it will be his no matter what his economic or social status; it will be his through political or religious upheavals and changes; it will be his for emotional release, and afford him an opportunity to com-mune with his fellow men, himself, and his Maker.

SECTION II

THE SECONDARY SCHOOL

The educational concept of music education at the secondary level should continue to include *all* pupils. It should provide a wide variety of musical offerings so that those especially talented may progress to their fullest capacity and so that every student, regardless of the amount of native talent, has an opportunity for musical experiences, both performance and appreciation.

Desirable attitudes, performance satisfactions, and sensitized listening will depend largely upon teaching techniques and materials used by teachers of music in the junior and senior high schools. It should be remembered that performance perfection serves the community as well as the school and the participating students, and further, that musical interests and abilities firmly established will carry over into adult life.

The following four chapters which deal with organization, techniques, and materials for grades seven through twelve, are based upon contemporary educational principles and practices applied to school music teaching.

PART I. ORGANIZATION, TECHNIQUES, AND PROCEDURES

PART II. COURSES AND CONTENT

12

ORGANIZATION AND ADMINISTRATION OF THE SECONDARY SCHOOL

The levels under special consideration in this chapter are grades seven to twelve inclusive, and are commonly referred to as the secondary school. These grades may be housed in different grade combinations, such as: junior high schools for grades seven, eight, and nine; senior high schools for grades ten, eleven, and twelve, or nine, ten, eleven, and twelve. It is believed quite generally that if the size of the school population warrants it, there are certain advantages in having the junior high school housed in a separate building and not combined with either the elementary nor senior high school. However, there are advantages to all types of grade combinations and many small communities have stressed these advantages successfully. The student and his musical development are the really important things to be considered here and this must be accomplished within the type of school which he attends.

The General Administrator. The excellence of the music program in the secondary school is directly related to the attitude towards music held by the superintendent and principal. It may be helpful if these administrators have had some musical training, but it is most important that they have an understanding of the fundamental aims of school music activities and actively support these beliefs. Most administrators are alert to demonstrated results and react to this much more readily than to arguments.

The Community. The individuals who comprise the community are interested in both values and costs. Actually, the school is an outgrowth of the needs and desires of the community as a whole. Parents always have found a way of paying for what they value most in the education of their children. If the adults of the community desire music of a high calibre in their high school, ways and means can be found to make this a reality.

Administrators and music teachers should be aware of the integrating service of music between the school and the entire community.

A few good demonstrations of this service can do more to gain community support for the school music program than any amount of talking. Support always has been a thing earned rather than demanded.

Curricular and Extra-Curricular Classification. The common differentiation made between curricular activities and those which are classed as extra-curricular is that the former are a regular part of the daily schedule of classes, that credit toward graduation is granted, and that the subject or activity is an integral part of the program of studies prescribed by school authorities; while the latter are voluntary, non-credit, non-required, and meet outside of the scheduled school day.

At one time in the early development of the school music program many musical organizations functioned as extra-curricular activities. This is true only in isolated instances today because wise and interested educators have recognized that if an activity is important for educational development, it is worthy of a place within the school day. A true extra-curricular activity may be defined as one which is a legitimate educative activity of the school which has not been provided for in the program of studies as yet.

Some items which have a definite bearing upon the curricular offerings are the size of the school district and the number of students enrolled, available rooms and equipment, the needs and interests of pupils and community, as well as the desires of the administration and the professional ambitiousness of the music teaching staff.

The School Day. Many important responsibilities of the music educator will demand time other than those hours within the school day. Some schools are making salary adjustments or giving other assistance when duties, often required by the school authorities, call for late afternoon, evening, or Saturday assignments. The regular music classes within the school day will be affected materially by the place they occupy in the over-all class schedule.

Length of Class Period. The starting time of the school day, length of lunch hour, time between classes, and dismissal time will vary according to such items as whether the majority of students are transported by bus, what proportion go home for lunch, distance students need to travel between classes, etc. It follows that these items would have a bearing upon the length of the class period. Most schools provide for home-room activities and assembly periods which need to be planned for within the six-hour school day.

A recent recommendation by the High School Curriculum Committee of the Music Educators National Conference is that administrators be urged to enlarge the school day to seven periods in order to take care of all types of music programs. This can be accomplished by, (a) shortening of the hour-long classes where they now exist, or by (b) lengthening the school day. There is a trend expressed by general educators that item (b) will eventually come into general practice.

A good schedule of classes, both as to length of period and number of periods per week should make it possible for all interested students to have an opportunity to participate in basic music activities for credit.

Music Credit. The usual practice for granting high school credit for music courses is that any music class which meets five times a week for a school year and which requires outside preparation equivalent to any academic subject, should receive one unit of credit. If outside preparation is not required, credit is usually granted on a laboratory basis, or one-half unit of credit. Two forty-five minute periods a week is considered a minimum for granting any credit and this generally carries one-fourth unit per school year.

In small schools where music courses are limited, a point system has been used effectively on the following basis.

(1) With no outside preparation required
  3 periods per week for one school year...................... 6 points
  2 periods per week for one school year...................... 4 points
(2) With outside preparation required
  3 periods per week for one school year......................12 points
  2 periods per week for one school year...................... 8 points
(3) Twenty points equivalent to one unit of credit

Credit for private study of music outside of school is usually on the basis of one-half unit of credit or ten points for one private lesson a week for a full school year with one hour daily practice.*

Size of Class. Some types of music activities flourish with large groups of students participating, with other types individual instruction is necessary. A balance between these two yield more than an average academic class pupil load. Several studies reveal that in terms of numbers of students taught, music is one of the least expensive in the entire secondary school curriculum.

Whether a music class carries credit or not, whether it is required or elective will help to decide what the most desirable size of the class should be. If both individual and group performance are to be engaged in, as in the general music class, it is desirable that the group should not exceed fifty members. As the required amount of individual attention increases, the class enrolment should decrease.

Additional discussion of class size will be found in subsequent chapters. It should be remembered that in starting a music program,

See Appendix C. for sample forms.

legitimate enthusiasm may stress numbers but this emphasis should be changed as rapidly as possible to include quality as well as numbers participating.

Housing and Equipment. The physical aspects which are conducive to successful teaching and which contribute to effective learning are the concern of both the general administrator and the music educator. The problems encountered usually involve sound proofing or wall absorption material, elevations, adequate size and shape of room, library and storage space, etc. These will be discussed in relation to specific music activities in later chapters. Any school planning new buildings or the remodeling of present facilities should consult a bulletin, "Music Rooms and Equipment", compiled by Clarence J. Best and sponsored by the Research Council of the Music Educators National Conference.

Records and Reports. The effective running of any school necessitates the keeping of records of enrolment, absences, and tardiness. Forms for admission, transfer, and special permissions need to be signed and filed. The larger the school, the more complicated the system of pupil accounting becomes. All kinds of cumulative records are valuable only if they are complete.

A competent music teacher will devise ways and means for accomplishing these details with a minimum of time and effort and thus cause no irritation to either himself or the administrative office. Attendance may be checked quickly by the use of seating charts and period attendance report blanks should be prepared so that the class is not interrupted. Much can be delegated to responsible students or class officers. The teacher who has his desk and register well organized at the very beginning of the term will save much time and confusion, and will greatly enhance his rating as an efficient teacher.

Supervision. According to modern school practices, the principal is responsible for the quality of instruction which takes place in the school building to which he is assigned. This could give rise to a problem for the music supervisor who has responsibility for the music classes but who feels a lack of authority to carry out his proposed program. In most instances where a subject supervisor is employed, a cooperative plan functions where the principal and supervisor jointly accept responsibility and support each other in authority.

Definition of Terms. The following definitions are quite universally accepted but often used erroneously.

(1) *Director* or *Directing Supervisor*—used in larger cities to indicate the chief supervisor. This individual is responsible for the coordination of the whole program of music and has many administrative duties.

(2) *Supervisor*—should be applied only to persons responsible for guiding the teaching of others.

(3) *Supervising Instructor*—indicates an individual who has instructional duties, but who combines with them the giving of help and guidance to other teachers.

(4) *Teacher* or *Instructor*—should be used for a person whose duties within the music department consist of the actual instruction of pupils.

(5) *Consultant or Resource Teacher*—should be applied to one who assists on call.

The Music Education Research Council Bulletin No. 18, titled "Music Supervision and Administration"* will answer many questions for the general administrator as well as those serving in the above five positions. It is suggested that all beginning music teachers study this material carefully.

*Music Educators National Conference, 64 East Jackson Blvd., Chicago, Illinois.

13   THE SECONDARY SCHOOL MUSIC TEACHER

In the days when the educational emphasis was placed upon subject matter instead of the development of the child, there was considerable conflict over the premise that a secondary school music teacher must be either a teacher of instrumental music or a teacher of vocal music. The stress was placed upon the medium or phase of music taught rather than upon the development of the student through the use of music.

It is assumed that each music educator will have at least one area, preferably two or more, where performance ability is acceptable, but to be successful a music educator must know something of both instrumental and vocal music literature and techniques. It should be remembered that music as a fundamental subject and art, is all inclusive. No one part may be isolated and treated as if it were not an integral part of the whole if the student is to be developed through the use of music as a whole.

The beginning school music teacher, for at least the first two or three years, usually serves in a comparatively small school system. The very nature of the organization of these schools makes it necessary for one teacher to be in charge of all music activities. How can a vocal specialist who has excluded instrumental music entirely for his training and background, or an instrumental specialist, who has ignored all vocal opportunities, be successful and effective in such a teaching assignment? It would follow that institutions preparing teachers of school music at the undergraduate level should see to it that their graduates are acquainted with, and prepared to teach at least the beginnings of all types of music activities *along with* a concentration in a major applied field.

Some administrators of small school systems try to off-set the deficiency of teacher training institutions by hiring teachers who are prepared to teach vocal music and an academic subject such as English or history, and to employ an instrumental teacher who can teach a few classes in science or mathematics. While this may solve some problems, it may create others. In the first place, there is a tendency to make a half-time music assignment into a two-thirds or a three-fourths assignment and leads too often to an over-loaded or crowded teaching schedule. Secondly, the music activities in a small school situation usually involve the same students and serious conflicts arise over which activity is more important or should have more advantageous scheduling. A successful music program should be an integrated one from the viewpoint of the student as well as from the angle of the subject, and where the half-time vocal music teacher and the half-time instrumental teacher have a basic concept of the over-all educational goal, the problem is minimized.

Personal Qualifications. An essential element in good teaching is human understanding. An ideal teacher will be interested primarily in the growth and development of the pupils he is instructing and is fully aware that *anything* which affects these pupils is a matter of importance.

A teacher who is teaching music solely as subject matter does not tend to improve but follows routines established by habit; while one interested in student growth is always seeking new ways and means for enrichment and often encounters the thrill of discovering latent or hidden talents. As all teaching may be considered a form of human service, the teacher must have a desire to understand his pupil as an individual, as a member of a group, and as a potential citizen.

Acceptable personal qualifications would include such items as a *pleasant attitude* which is positive instead of negative; *reliability* or dependability˙ so that unwavering confidence is ever present; *sincerity* which reflects an honesty of mind and intention; *industry* which stems from intelligent steadfastness and habitual diligence; *tact* which comes from a delicate, sympathetic perception and gives an adroitness in successfully meeting the requirements of a situation; *initiative* which demonstrates energy and aptitude to introduce courses of action; *willingness* construed to mean desirous of and ready to perform duties not only required but beyond the terms of contract; *imagniation* connoting the exercise of plastic or creative powers; and, *cooperativeness* which has the aspects of modesty and welcomes opportunity to operate jointly with one or more·persons in a collective action for mutual benefit.

The above personal qualifications may cause one to feel that nothing short of a paragon will suffice. It is conceded that 'teachers are human beings' and it follows that the secondary school music teacher should demonstrate the human qualities which are characteristic of all men by being sympathetic, compassionate, and aware of human frailties.

Educational Qualifications. There are three major areas of educational pursuit for a secondary school music teacher, namely: (a) music, which includes applied music or personal performance proficiency, (b) education or teaching techniques, both general and specifically for the teaching of music, and (c) cultural or academic subjects, which contribute to the general background of the individual. References should be consulted for specific courses for the training of music educators.

Seven Major Areas of Proficiency. A centering of attention on the following areas of proficiency will be helpful to those who are teaching or preparing to teach music in any school and especially at the secondary school level.

I. The Sociological Significance of Music

The culture of a people varies in direct proportion with a rapidly changing social order. It is possible that the change in objectives of music education has been brought about partially by the socio-economic upheaval. The true significance of music sociologically is not from the economic basis alone but rather from the basis of human elements. The sociological values of group participation has long been demonstrated and is taken for granted.

Modern living demands that the school assume many of the sociological functions once taken care of by the church and home. This demand should not be decried but met intelligently. All of us have seen the joy and satisfaction which accompany the ease of a truly socially-integrated personality. A person cannot be called socially anemic if he has the talent to perform musically for the pleasure of others or if he has the training which equips him to carry a tune as part of a musical group. This sociological responsibility of music teaching is not delayed but is immediate and very definitely indicated. The thinking and practices of music educators must be pointed towards these progressive ends.

II. A Functioning Psychology

A purposive psychology rather than a mechanistic one is needed to cope with school music problems, and a functioning rather than a theoretical psychology is imperative. Psychology has pointed for a long time to the qualities inherent in the original nature of man. Are music educators guilty of curbing these dominating innate tendencies rather than utilizing them? Are teachers of school music justified in attempting to eliminate entirely the physical appeal of music and to utilize only the aesthetic and intellectual appeal?

It has been granted for a long time that music acts as an emotional stabilizer but do secondary school music teachers take this fact into account and create situations where it can function to the best advantage?

88

III. An Educational Philosophy

One's philosophy of music education is controlled by one's philosophy of all education and is in reality one's philosophy of life. This philosophy must reach wide horizons, it must include the dull and the superior student with their lives viewed as a whole; it must include the community in terms of the individual and as a unit; it must reach our nation and all humanity with a complete realization that music is a dominant force in the life of every living person.

A philosophy is an intimate, personal thing, and each music teacher should analyze his own to be certain that it rises above irritating trivialities. Do students who are prospective music teachers have a well defined philosophy of education which they wholeheartedly accept and practice?

IV. Personal Adequacy

As intangible as desirable personality may be, many of the component parts are very recognizable and it has been proved beyond a doubt that many phases of a desirable personality can be developed. Personal adequacy means acceptable personal appearance, neatness, cleanliness, and appropriateness, which must be practiced as well as preached. It includes proper attitudes in regard to work, students, fellow teachers, administrators, and the community. Such attitudes must have sincerity as their beginning. Personal adequacy extends to the very important ability of making a correct personal approach and this is closely allied with desirable personality, personal appearance, and proper attitudes. A poor personal approach always proves to be a handicap. Shall these items be neglected in the training of music educators?

V. A Scientific Attitude

A truly scientific attitude is one of inquiry and evaluation. It is not a search for data to uphold the opinions already held but a sincere desire to know and be directed toward the truth by impersonal and unbiased findings. Those in training who will carry on the music education profession should possess a scientific attitude, be equipped with a skilful technique, with an ability to administer, devise, and revise scientific materials, and most important of all, with an understanding of how to correctly interpret and apply the findings. Science cannot take the place of art but the arts can be improved and enhanced by the use of science.

VI. An Educational Goal

We have reached the place where the goal of music education can be defined as the sensitizing of every individual to a realization of music to the fullest of its meaning and loveliness. Our effort to reach this goal must be sincere. Everyone should re-read the "Statement of Belief and Purpose" of the Music Educators National Conference.* If this is comprehended and accepted, our music education goal will reach into life and not stop at the end of a course or the passing of a certain test. Once this educational goal is clearly in mind, the next step is to adopt a workable plan whereby this goal may be achieved.

VII. Performance Proficiency

During the early days of school music, the teacher was primarily a performing musician. In a subsequent period, emphasis was placed upon teaching ability rather than sufficient performance ability. At the present time, even greater demands are made but demands that are justified because they ask for more than a mere balance between teaching ability and performance ability. Music educators should strive for perfection in both areas because ours is a duo-profession. This demand will eliminate automatically those persons who are technically inefficient as well as those who are pedagogically incapable. This demand can be met only by the elimination of students in training who show conclusively their inability or their lack of capacity to acquire and achieve.

This elimination should take place not at the completion of an unsuccessful first year of teaching, which is such a sad experience for pupils, the training institution, and the teacher involved; it should not take place after graduation by the withholding of a recommendation for a position but rather during the freshman year in college where students still have time to adjust themselves and to elect other fields where the requirements are not so exacting or where special talent is not a necessity. A recent research study revealed that on a basis of fifteen items, the ultimate success in music education courses, measured in terms of grades, could be predicted with a high degree of success.**

*See Appendix A.
**"The Ability Pattern of Senior College Students Majoring in Music Education at the University of Minnesota," Ph.D. Thesis. University of Minnesota. Hazel Nohavec Morgan. 1943. Available on micro-film.

Summary. The challenge which is to be met by teacher training institutions is to supply the demand for talented, capable, intelligent, cultured, and self-controlled teachers of music, who will dare to be individual, and who will look for sociological, psychological, and scientific aids; teachers with a definite philosophy which will carry them through to a realization of their ultimate goal; teachers who will strive for technical perfection and who, because they have a realization that music uninhabited by spirit tends to deteriorate with startling rapidity, will not let this perfection take the place of the necessity for a development of the inner energies. This challenge to supply the demand for music teachers who will be fit guardians of the trust which all education has laid at the feet of school music is large, but it *can* be met. A Condensed Statement of the Code of the National Education Association follows.

The teacher should be courteous, just, and professional in all relationships.

Desirable ethical standards require cordial relations between teacher and pupil, home and school.

The conduct of the teacher should conform to the accepted patterns of behavior of the most wholesome members of the community.

The teacher should strive to improve educational practice through study, travel, and experimentation.

Unfavorable criticism of associates should be avoided except when made to proper officials.

Testimonials regarding the teacher should be truthful and confidential.

Membership and active participation in local, state, and national professional associations are expected.

The teacher should avoid indorsement of all educational materials for personal gain.

Great care should be taken by the teacher to avoid interference between other teachers and pupils.

Fair salary schedules should be sought and when established carefully upheld by all professionals.

No teacher should knowingly underbid a rival for a position.

No teacher should accept a compensation for helping another teacher to get a position or a promotion.

Honorable contracts when signed should be respected by both parties and dissolved only by mutual consent.

Official business should be transacted only through properly designated officials.

The responsibility for reporting all matters harmful to the welfare of the school rests upon each teacher.

Professional growth should be stimulated through suitable recognition and promotion within the ranks.

Unethical practices should be reported to local, state, or national commissions on ethics.

The term "teacher" as used here includes all persons directly engaged in educational work.

TEACHING TECHNIQUES AND CLASSROOM CONTROL

Most problems which confront new teachers, or experienced ones for that matter, involve one or all of the following, (a) a knowledge of *what* should be taught, (b) a knowledge of techniques for teaching, or *how* to present the *what*, and (c) a knowledge of class control, or how to maintain a learning situation.

Teacher education institutions usually succeed in equipping their graduates with academic knowledge and an acquaintance with literature for the various music activities found at the secondary level. The methods of procedure to be used are of prime importance but there is no one technique which can be specified as a panacea for all ills, and no set of rules or routines which can be guaranteed to bring about perfect results at all times in all situations with all students. It should be remembered constantly that teaching is not a routine process even though specific routines are used. Any technique may be called a good one if it produces desirable results, that is, produces artistic singing and playing, real power in sight reading, and establishes enjoyment and satisfaction.

The procedure used is dependent upon:

1. The Teacher
    a. Ability
    b. Training and experience
    c. Philosophy
    d. Knowledge of psychology
    e. Knowledge of general teaching methods
2. The Pupils
    a. Previous experience and training
    b. Ability
    c. General attitude
3. The Material
    a. Difficulty   b. Amount   c. Familiarity
4. The Physical Equipment
5. The Desired Outcomes.

What Should Be Taught

Courses of Study. Most State Departments of Education have prepared outlines and suggested listings for the information and guidance of teachers in all areas, including music. Those which have been issued during the past few years are from the viewpoint of the place of music in the entire school program and are in keeping with accepted present-day practices. They usually contain a statement of objectives and suggested minimum accomplishments. A teacher beginning work in a new state should investigate the Course of Study issued by that state.

Basic Music Textbooks. Certain types of music classes or courses center their work about a selected basic text. It is important for the teacher to investigate the general content of the book and be informed as to how the authors or editors intended their material to be used. It is not intended here to indicate that these editorial instructions, suggestions, or techniques be followed without deviation or adaptation.

The Starting Level of Difficulty. Students attending secondary schools come from various elementary schools. Their experience with music will vary with the program of music which was set up in these elementary schools. It is not uncommon to find a few who have had little or no music instruction beyond the singing of a few rote songs, and also to find a few who, due to special talents or privileges, are already well along the way to a professional career. However, many students entering the secondary school will have achieved the levels of attainments indicated in Chapter X. It should be remembered that it is not the fault of the child if he has not attained the techniques and abilities which you think he should have when he enters your class. Rather, it is your job to discover his real and present level of accomplishment and procede from there.

The singing of a few songs or the playing of a few marches, some old and some new, will reveal the reading level of the group, familiarity with literature, technical difficulties, etc. A question period or brief oral quiz of only five minutes in length will yield an index to the class knowledge of the basic mechanics of music such as note and rest values, rhythmic patterns, key names, etc. A seeming lack should be no cause for alarm, it may be due partially to 'vacation retrogression' and can be refreshed by incidental teaching along with the new music being taught.

Major Interest of Individual Student. It would be ideal if early in the term the teacher could have a short individual conference with each student so that special interests and abilities could be known. This would aid in many ways but especially it would establish an *esprit de corps* between teacher and pupil, and would let the teacher do better guidance for selective and special music groups. The large number of students in each class, full teaching schedules, and limited hours in the day, make such scheduled conferences for all students practically impossible. A sincere desire for this information on the part of the teacher will make for alertness to opportunities which may come before class, after class, on the campus or street, or any occasion where informal chatting may be done. The approach should be one of friendliness rather than inquisitiveness.

The secret of interest in most music activities has its roots in the theory of contagion. If you are genuinely pleased, radiant, enthusiastic, and interested in music and the development of students through music, this will be caught by all with whom you come in contact. Secondary school students think they are adults, and in many respects are very mature. It is wise to regard each student as an individual who is very worth while and who has at least the potentials to contribute to fruitfulness and pleasure.

Teaching Techniques

Teaching techniques have been compared to a quiver full of arrows. If one arrow is used and it does not hit the mark, another one should be ready instantly, and another, and another, until the point you are trying to put across is comprehended by all. Techniques should not be regarded as *good* or *bad,* but rather as *effective* or *ineffective* in a specific situation with a specific group of children.

It is presupposed that certificated teachers have a working knowledge of the 'laws of learning', a knowledge of applied psychology, and a knowledge of child development and maturity, for these all influence the type of teaching technique to be used. Often new techniques will need to be developed in order to meet specific or unique situations and there should be no hesitancy to experiment with new ones, nor to discard if proven inadequate.

Such items as previous experience, heredity, environment, maturity, and individual differences; as well as understandings, satisfactions, attitudes, skills, and appreciations will influence the process of learning and therefore have a bearing upon the teaching technique used.

Regardless of the specific technique of presentation to be used, it is of paramount importance that all teachers, and especially those working in music, have a full realization that, "Items within any given learning situation should have some relationship to each other, and all of them must be related to some whole which is the real reason for the given learning situation".* Anything which is apart from use in a meaningful situation is meaningless.

*"The Guidance of Learning Activities." William H. Burton. Appleton-Century-Croft, Inc. New York, 1944. Page 126.

Numerous studies have been made in an effort to isolate *a* technique which is good or effective from every angle. These have resulted in two general conclusions.

(1) There is no one technique which is desirably productive for all teachers at all times for all subjects with all students.

(2) The result of good teaching can be identified and measured to a considerable degree. Therefore it is well to know that skill in asking questions, well developed assignments, knowledge of subject matter, effective appraisal of progress, use of illustrative materials; along with general appreciation, democratic attitude, freedom from disciplinary problems, and a conversational person-to-person manner, are all closely identified with a desirable teaching and learning situation.

Classroom Procedure

The two phases of classroom procedure to be discussed here are organization and control. If these are well managed, the stage is set to make full use of the time spent together and which will be conducive to maximum progress.

Classroom Organization. The simple details of classroom organization such as taking the roll, reporting absences, etc., should be reduced to a routine so that they are accomplished quickly and in a proper fashion. The reasons for this routine are:

(1) It saves time for more important activities.

(2) It relegates mechanics to its proper proportion of significance in relation to the over-all time at disposal for class.

(3) It prevents disorders from starting.

Many school systems have set policies in regard to the mechanics of class organization, and the teacher should adhere to these rigidly if for no other reason than to demonstrate cooperation. Administrators often complain that teachers of music are especially remiss in this particular thing.

Items which lend themselves readily to routine procedures and responsibility for which can be delegated to student assistants are:

(1) *Recording attendance.* Regular seats or places should be assigned at the first class meeting. This arrangement will be controlled by such factors as the size of the class, size and shape of the room, type of music activity, and the personal preference of the teacher; all decided on the basis of what is best for the over-all learning situation. Consideration should be shown for unique physical needs, such as exceptionally tall or short pupils, seeing deficiencies, etc. With a seating chart on the desk, the vacant places may be noted during the first musical selection.

(2) *Distribution and collection of music materials.* Selections to be used may be listed on the blackboard where the librarian and all students may observe. If the time is short between classes meeting in the same room, this listing should be prepared on a card or piece of paper which is placed in a selected place, perhaps on the teacher's desk, where an assigned student may take it and write the material on the blackboard during the first selection. To save untold confusion of material, only one or two librarians should have access to the music library.

Some schools have found the use of shelving racks advantageous where students may take a book or folder of music as they pass on the way to their assigned seat, and return them when leaving the room.

(3) *Arrangement of chairs, music racks, etc.* This need not be time consuming nor unduly noisy, and may be handled by each student taking responsibility for his own, or by a set-up committee which can be in the room a few minutes before the opening of the rehearsal. (See Chapter XVIII.)

(4) *Adjustment of heat, light, ventilation, and certain pieces of equipment.* If there are regulations for the entire building concerning these items, the music room should be no exception. Sixty-eight degrees is regarded quite universally as a satisfactory classroom temperature and any variation of five degrees above or below this will affect the amount and the quality of the work done. If the humidity is in excess of 50, it will usually cause lessening of attention and achievement.

Artificial illumination, with shades and reflectors used when needed, along with various modern lighting devices aid in the proper distribution of light. The location of windows, the building location of the room, size and shape of room, color of walls, and the specific music activity, all should be taken into consideration for lighting intensity. Light which produces a glare on a smooth or glazed surface, especially music paper, should be avoided and students with defective vision must be seated to their individual advantage. Thoughtlessly teachers will stand in front of a window and thereby cause students to look directly into the source of light. Lights on music racks should be hooded so that what helps one student does not interfere with another one.

All miscellaneous equipment to be used in any specific class should be in place and in working order before the class begins if time is to be saved and disorder averted. This means blackboard space, chalk, erasers, reproducing machines, etc.

(5) *General appearance of the room.* Neatness, cleanliness, color and simplicity of arrangement add to the general attractiveness of the music room. These have more effect upon work habits and

attitude than most teachers realize. Occasional changes are desirable and students, if given the opportunity, will take initiative and aid in keeping the music room one of the most attractive, pleasing, and interesting in the entire building.

Classroom Control or Discipline

The word *discipline* literally means "treatment of a learner", which means that there are positive as well as negative aspects, also, that there are disciplines which originate within the individual as well as those imposed upon him from without. Harl R. Douglass states that, "the goal of discipline is neither perfect order and respect at all costs, nor the freedom of pupils to do as they please, but the guiding of pupils to do what they should without too much compulsion and always with a keen eye on the long-time effects upon the individual".* It would follow, then, that those who are engaged in teaching should be interested primarily in disciplines which have educational values.

Assuming that the music teacher is well disciplined in the broad sense of the word, the discussion to follow will deal with classroom control from the angle of adequate teacher-pupil relationship.

Discipline or classroom control has been and still is the worry of many teachers, both experienced and inexperienced. It is unique that the ability to manage groups of children seemingly does not improve with experience in proportion to the improvement which experience gives to other facets of teaching. The purpose served by disciplinary measures may be briefly stated as the establishment and maintenance of desirable situations where distractions, disturbances, and misbehaviors are absent or at a minimum.

Most undesirable disciplinary situations would be avoided or averted by the removal of temptation or opportunity for misbehavior. It is a proven fact that things are accomplished through order and discipline, it is the methods to be used in achieving this order which causes the most difficulty for music teachers. Education has traveled a long way from rigid rules and regulations, harsh and cruel punishment, and arbitrary respect demanded for authority, to the present day where the emphasis is upon the development of valid and reliable controls of self-discipline. It is hoped that all music teachers will use careful analyzation as a substitute for anger, fear, and tempermental explosions which are indications of lack of self-discipline on the part of the teacher.

*"Organization and Administration of Secondary Schools." Harl R. Douglass. Ginn and Company, Boston, Massachusetts. 1945, page 284.

Types of Punishment. Regardless of the use of sound techniques, situations will arise which call for action. There are many types and degrees of punishment used for unconventional behavior. Perhaps the most primitive type is vindication which has its inception in vengeance. This has no place in the classroom or anywhere else. The next in order is retribution which seems to be based upon the law of 'cause and effect' where misbehavior is followed by natural punishment. There may be occasions when a teacher will need to see to it that unpleasantness or discomfort follow when undesirable things are done. This should lead logically to an awareness on the part of the pupil of consequences which will follow *unfailingly.*

Various disciplinary methods have their roots in humiliation such as wearing a dunce cap. The fear of humiliation is almost as fatal as the actual abasement and leads only to suppression rather than a recognition of the necessity on the part of the pupil to really do what he ought to do.

Substitution often proves a wise course and belongs to the positive phase of discipline. This is illustrated by the small child putting beans in his nose. It does no good to shout, "Don't put beans in your nose", because he has no realization of the consequences. But the danger is averted if he is given something else to play with which is more interesting. This method is very useful when the misdeeds are the result of the child's total life history (heredity, environment and previous training).

Research and democratic thinking gives assurance that prevention is much the wisest course. Most undersirable or anti-social behavior *can* be prevented but it takes intelligence, understanding, and a knowledge of remedial measures. Any student who realizes the advantages of acceptable behavior will cease to be a discipline problem.

Some Causes of Misbehavior. The chief causes of misbehavior will fall into one or more of the following.

1. Desire to attract attention.
2. Fatigue or other forms of bodily discomfort.
3. Undirected energy.
4. Slow classroom tempo.
5. Intangible causes.

Any teacher should be able to identify the problems which fall into the first three categories and the treatment is relatively simple. Item four is the fault of inadequate lesson planning and the use of poor teaching techniques on the part of the teacher. Intangible causes, item five, need the services of an experienced analyst because they are deep seated and this is the only area where grave concern is justifiable. It should be remembered that a real inability to behave is closely associated with an inability to learn because they may stem from identical or related causes.

Pupil Reaction to Certain Control Measures. Constructive control or discipline works through educative processes which develop a sensitivity to law and order based upon understanding. Some few students do not respond to constructive control and make other steps necessary.

(1) *Threats vs. Warnings.* A threat is an expression of intention to inflict punishment and usually is received as a dare by the student. Therefore it is an unwise technique to use because it carries with it a promise which must be fulfilled. A warning is a cautionary measure and serves as a reminder that consequences could ensue. Warnings often can be conveyed by a shake of the head or a look from the corner of the eye which lets the student know that you are aware of what is taking place. Such remarks as, ''I'm surprised at you'', or ''Are you really thinking?'', said quietly and only to the offender, will serve to show that the teacher expects proper behavior and is a trifle disgusted. Warnings should not give the impression that the act is disturbing or upsetting to the teacher because this admtis to the student that the teacher's control is slipping, also.

(2) *Personal Loyalty.* The personality of the teacher often stirs loyalty or a form of youthful hero-worship. If control is completely personalized, the results achieved will tend to be temporary and last only so long as that particular teacher is in charge, with the pupil reacting negatively to other teachers. If desirable attitudes are maintained, this is a legitimate and useful form of control and can merit fine student reaction. There is a close relationship between loyalty and respect for authority. Respect is an outcome of excellent leadership and is like affection, in that it is earned and deserved rather than demanded.

(3) *Apologies.* If an honest and sincere apology is offered, it should be accepted graciously and the spirit which prompted its giving should be commended. A forced or demanded apology is usually mere forced hypocricy and the student reacts with intensified (because it is unexpressed) antagonism and resentfulness.

(4) *Opinions of Classmates.* Standards of behavior for both individuals and groups are dependent upon 'public opinion'. This is a very slow developmental process but it does determine the level of behavior. The approval of classmates is much more important to a student than the approval of the teacher. It even may be necessary at times to curb some of the ruthless criticism which takes place among members of a class. Harsh criticism from those of similar age is accepted with an entirely different reaction than

if the same words of criticism were given by the teacher. Harsh criticism should be avoided and sarcasm will not be used by good music teachers.

(5) *Corporal Punishment.* This corrective measure is rarely used in secondary schools. The reasons are obvious, it is not effective at this age level and never fails to arouse a feeling of martyrdom. If the situation has progressed, perhaps through the unwise use of threats, to a place where corporal punishment must be used, be very sure that all state laws and local regulations are complied with fully. Proof of guilt beyond all doubt and the admission of failure of other methods should precede any administration of corporal punishment.

(6) *Call for Assistance.* Only when the situation is beyond control by the teacher, or when school regulations require that specific infractions be reported, should pupils be sent to the office or parents be called in for conference.

Complaints, justifications, and defenses set up by parents should be received tactfully and investigated thoroughly. Usually only chronic and major offenders are involved when necessary to call for assistance. Be sure that the results will be a strengthening of confidence and goodwill among parents, faculty, and student.

(7) *Suspension and Expulsion.* The difference between suspension and expulsion is only one of duration, suspension being temporary exclusion while expulsion is permanent. On rare occasions situations may arise where one or the other of these methods is the only choice. The situation would be one of serious offences which have become chronic or incurable, and should be used only after consultation by administrator and parents. They should be used as a last recourse when all other methods have failed because it publicly labels a student and may produce reactions which will have a definite effect upon the future life pattern of the student.

(8) *All for One.* One of the corrective techniques often used by music teachers is reproof directed at the entire class. Naturally, if the whole class as a unit is out of order this may be what is needed. However, such a situation is rare because the difficulty invariably centers around one or a very few individuals. The scolding of the entire class for the infraction of a few is a very bad practice from many viewpoints, especially: (a) this is not practicing isolation of the problem, (b) the innocent are helpless and resent the implication that the teacher thinks they are guilty, and (c) the offender escapes as being only partially responsible.

(9) *Benefit of Doubt.* Much may be accomplished by giving the benefit of doubt to a student because it lets the student 'save face' and enhances the prestige of the teacher. If the infraction is slight, often a remark such as, "I'm sure you didn't intend to

do that", will minimize the situation and cause the student to desire to live up to your estimation of him. No child thrives when he feels that the teacher dislikes him as a person, the things he does and says may be disliked but the student, himself, should and can be liked, always.

The technique of ignoring is one of the finest and is suitable for most minor disturbances. This does not mean acceptance nor approval, but a good teacher knows that slight misbehaviors grow in importance as soon as attention is called to them. Constant reproof savors of nagging, disrupts the class, wastes time, is ineffective, and creates an unhealthy learning situation. And further, this refusal to be nettled demonstrates the personal control of the teacher.

Summary

The true basis for desirable control lies in good teaching techniques and simple mechanics of routine for they will keep disorder at a minimum and will be conducive to the development of student self-control. Judgment is the outgrowth of analyzed experiences and should be sought by every music teacher in all teacher-pupil relationships which concern classroom organization and classroom control.

15 THE SECONDARY SCHOOL MUSIC CURRICULUM

The general educational patterns and objectives for the curriculums of all secondary schools should be investigated as a preface to any study of a specific area curriculum such as music. Any curriculum or program of courses should be flexible to a considerable extent because it exists for the purpose of the development of the potentialities which are inherent in the students served and must be amenable to the capacities of these students.

Curriculum content, *per se,* has received much consideration and its importance warrants continued investigation. The crux of the situation involves activities, experiences, and desirable outcomes as opposed to factual content. Development of the following attributes need to be uppermost in the thinking of those music educators responsible for the content of secondary school music curriculums.

1. Group consciousness which leads to an awareness of the things involved in living happily and effectively with others.
2. Critical and evaluating thinking based upon experience and information.
3. Emotional stability which comes as a result of practiced control.
4. Acceptable attitudes toward cooperation and helpfulness.
5. An awareness of individual and personal responsibility to be of service.
6. Acceptable behavior as an individual and as a part of a group.
7. A sensitivity to beauty and loveliness which demands association with the fine arts for personal satisfaction.
8. A philosophy and spirituality which originates within and radiates outward.

All of the above items will be outcomes of the acquiring of knowledges and skills if the basic music curriculum is properly constructed and the teacher works for their furtherance.

The content of any secondary school curriculum reflects the philosophy of the music staff which has devised it. While the director of music or head supervisor may serve as counselor and perhaps supply a major portion of the inspiration, the end product should be a fusion of the experiences of children, classroom teachers, special music teachers, and administrators if the curriculum is to be vital, effective, and adequate for the specific secondary school situation for which it was organized.

102

Curriculum Revisions. The study which eventually results in the revision of a curriculum is a continuous thing and demands time and patience. It should be neither hurried nor sporadic. Changes should be made on the basis of analysis of results over a sufficiently long period of use. Drastic alterations made on evidences from immediate or short term experimentation usually are undesirable. However, revisions are necessary if demands made by changing conditions are to be met.

Those responsible for curriculum revisions will need to weigh their answers to the following questions.

1. To what extent should music be required or elective, and what specific music activities or classes should be required, elective, or selective?
2. What provisions need to be made for an equitable balance between vocal and instrumental music, and listening activities?
3. What type of material is best suited to the specific grade level?
4. Is integration with other school subjects desirable and feasible? Can provision for this be made?
5. Can ample provision be made for articulation of elementary grades with the junior high school, and junior high school with the senior high school?

There will be additional questions important in local situations which will require answers.

OUTLINE OF PROGRAM FOR MUSIC EDUCATION IN SECONDARY SCHOOLS

The following is a bare outline of areas of instruction which can serve as a skeleton framework for the construction of a music curriculum for junior and senior high schools. It is the result of considered thinking of a large number of outstanding and experienced music educators.

Areas of Instruction: Junior High School, Grades VII, VIII, and IX

1. General Course in Music
2. Vocal Music
   a. Choral Groups　　　　b. Small Ensembles
3. Instrumental Music
   a. Orchestra　　　　c. Small Ensembles
   b. Band　　　　d. Class Instrumental Instruction
      e. Applied Music Study (for credit in Grade IX)
4. Relating and Coordinating Out-of-School Influences with those of the Classroom. This to include Radio, Television, Motion Pictures, Civic Music Organizations, Church, and Home.

Areas of Instruction: Senior High School, Grades X, XI, and XII*

1. General Course in Music—An Appreciation Activity Course Open to All Students.
2. Vocal Music
   - a. Choral Groups
   - b. Small Ensembles
   - c. Class Voice Instruction
   - d. Applied Music Study for Credit
3. Instrumental Music
   - a. Orchestra
   - b. Band
   - c. Small Ensembles
   - d. Class Instrumental Instruction
   - e. Applied Music Study for Credit
4. A Listening Course in the Literature and History of Music—A course which will emphasize the relationship between music and the other fine arts.
5. Theoretical Studies in Music.

Areas for Elementary and Secondary Schools

1. Assembly Music Programs
   - a. Singing by all the pupils
   - b. Appearance of school music organizations
   - c. Appearance of outside musical artists
2. Recitals and Concerts by Student Performers
3. Educational Concerts
4. Musical Programs in the Community

The following four chapters deal specifically with selected phases of the above outline of studies, namely, the General Music Class, Vocal Music, Instrumental Music, and other Music Classes, with direct application to the secondary school level.

*From MENC Publication.

16 THE GENERAL MUSIC CLASS

A realization that only approximately one-fourth of all secondary school students are enrolled in bands, orchestras, and choruses, so called performing groups, has given rise to a strong movement to provide a course in music which would be profitable for the entire student body. For a long time it has been felt that the music offerings, especially at the senior high school level, were designed to serve only those who have special talent and performance skills. It will be granted readily that those secondary students who do not have the necessary qualifications for membership in selected music organizations need and could profit by continued instruction and contact with music. The important questions are what to present, how to present it, and where to find teachers with adequate background to teach such a class.

Description. Mursell states that "general music is the trunk of a developmental program of music education, not just a course at a certain level, and various specialties (orchestra, chorus, band, etc.) are its branches".* The approach to the content as well as the teaching techniques used should be positive in nature and not dominantly technical.

Basically, any general music class would consist of a logical sequence of activities, experiences, and learnings planned to develop comprehensive and many-sided musical growth. The emphasis would be on awareness, initiative, discrimination, and information, as well as performance skill commensurate with ability. The end product would be a well developed responsiveness to music as an art form and as a utility art.

In considering the general music class as an integral part of the secondary school music program, the word *general* should be interpreted as 'having wide value and appeal'. Under no circumstance should it be regarded as an outlet or catch-all for misfits, or those students not wanted elsewhere.

The Junior High School. At the junior high school level general administrators are quite agreed that the importance of the graphic and fine arts is such as to merit a place in the required curriculum. For many years it has been almost a universal practice to have

*James L. Mursell. *Education for Musical Growth*, Ginn and Co., Boston, 1948. Page 65.

general music class attendance required for students in grades seven and eight, but elective in grade nine. Due to lack of planning or vision, these required courses have been conducted usually as an extension of the music period as found in the elementary grades rather than broadening to include all phases of music with emphasis on the needs and special interests of the students who comprise the specific class being taught.

It is regretable that in some instances this class has become a record playing session with no thought of directed listening on the part of the teacher nor active participation on the part of the students. While listening is one of the important phases of music and should be adequately presented, by no means is it the only phase which can be presented to a heterogeneous group in a junior high school general music class.

The Senior High School. Some senior high schools are programming courses in the area of the allied arts of at least one semester in length and given under the tutelage of specialists in each art. The communicative arts such as architecture, drama, radio and television arts, painting, sculpture, dance, and music, are the ones logically included. This course is general in nature and music occupies an important place in the over-all course plan, in fact, music usually serves as the integrating medium for the entire course.

Many senior high schools offer a course in general music under such titles as *Music for Enjoyment, Music for Everyone,* etc., in an effort to increase its attractiveness or to counteract any unpopularity which may have become attached to the term *General Music* through poorly selected content and the use of inadvisable methods of presentation.

Course Content Suggestions. It should be re-emphasized here that no standard content can or should be stipulated for accomplishment in any general music class because this would tend to defeat the real purpose of the offering. The previous musical experiences and present musical interests of those taking such a course will center around or cut across some of the following items.

I. *Unit Themes or Central Topics.* Any unit or area of intensification which has its origin within the student group is more vital than one superimposed by teacher decision or dictate. For example: it was learned through informal sources that a certain student member of a general music class could strum some chords on a guitar. This particular student had been a nuisance at times and was regarded by some faculty members as a 'problem case'. He was surprised at the sincere interest and commendation shown by the teacher, his ego and importance in the group rose appreciably.

It was a very logical step to present and talk about folk tunes, cowboy songs, the place of the guitar in the westward movement, and to listen to recordings made by such artists as Segovia. It also was a logical lead into the investigation of other string instruments and to composed literature, starting with music based upon folk tunes.

The following list of topics may suggest possible areas which would have an appeal to the students of most average general music classes.

1. Music of Our Allies
2. Music of American Indians
3. Music of the Mountains
4. Music of the Plains and Prairies
5. Music of Rivers and the Sea
6. Music That Tells a Story
7. Dance Forms in Music
8. Primitive Musical Instruments
9. Music of the South
10. Music of American Composers (French, German, Russian, etc.)
11. Music of Living Composers
12. From "Jazz to Symphony"
13. Music of the 17th Century (18th, 19th, 20th)

II. *Singing.* The singing of songs which make an appeal through lilting melody and strong rhythmic flow afford a good starting place. Unison songs are always popular even when the group is capable of singing in parts. If the boys' voices are unstable, the use of S.A.B. arrangements with the tune in the baritone are appealing. It should be remembered that singing is a natural approach and may lead logically to all other phases of music study.

Attention may be directed to pronunciation, enunciation, and even the fundamentals of tone production, so as to give an understanding of the possibilities of the use of the voice.

III. *Listening.* There should be a definite purpose for every recorded selection presented. This purpose may be to illustrate voice or instrument tone quality, musical form, sheer beauty of tones in combination, critical evaluation, the telling of a story, and many, many, others. The exact purpose should be known by both teacher and pupil.

IV. *Playing.* The playing of instruments will be largely a matter of accompaniments to singing. Chording at the piano is stressed and explained in several recent music text books which have been designed especially for use by average secondary school students. If sufficient performing talent is present, occasional recitals or student concerts may be presented at the general music class time but prepared outside of school hours.

V. *Dancing.* The popularity of folk dancing and the ease with which it can be presented is a fine adjunct to the study of all folk music. Bodily response to rhythm is splendid in the furtherance of music as a living art at this age.

VI. *Creating.* The writing of additional appropriate stanzas to songs sung, the designing of words to simple instrumental selections, or the actual writing of both words and music may develop within certain musical units of study. (See Chapter VII.)

Time Allotment. A minimum of ninety minutes per week should be allotted to a general music class and this time should be in not fewer than two periods per week.

Class Size. The general music class should not exceed the size of scheduled courses in other fields which have similar objectives. The average enrolment should be approximately forty or fifty students. This is large enough to be adequate for effective choral singing and small enough to give some individual assistance.

Materials and Equipment. Access to an adequate library of music and music reference books is quite imperative. All types of illustrative material as well as audio-visual equipment, add to the effectiveness of presentation.

Conclusion. A general music class which has been well planned and taught by a well-prepared and enthusiastic teacher will have many values among which will be well-balanced musical development with real musical significance for all enrolled. In places where effective general music classes are a part of the regular music curriculum, there has ensued a marked increase in interest in the so-called performance activities, such as band, chorus, orchestra, and ensembles.

17 VOCAL MUSIC IN SECONDARY SCHOOLS

It has been demonstrated in the elementary grades that all children accept and enjoy music unless they have had unfortunate experiences with musical activities. This premise is especially true of junior and senior high school students. If accepted and progressive techniques of instruction are used and suitable materials are selected, the musical abilities and interests established in the elementary grades will flower in profusion in the secondary schools.

In addition to the singing which is a part of the General Music Class discussed in Chapter XVI, various standard types of vocal classes will be found in most secondary schools. Items such as the size of the community, how long vocal music has been included in the specific school curriculum, the attitude and interest of the school administrators and community, as well as the effectiveness of the school music teacher, will be apparent by the local emphasis given certain types of vocal activity. Ideally, the vocal needs of the student body, individually and collectively, should be the determining factor. This chapter will be concerned with choirs, choruses, glee clubs, voice classes and small vocal ensembles.

Membership in these choral groups will be on either an elective basis, where the student chooses to become a member; or on a selective basis, where certain requirements must be met after the student has indicated a desire to 'try-out' for membership.

The chief reasons for offering these various vocal music activities in addition to any required music class, is to provide further instruction for the more gifted and interested students and produce performing groups which are a satisfaction to the students, a credit to the school, and service to the community.

It is recognized that there will be some differentiation among the vocal groups at the junior and senior high school levels. The following discussion should apply to the majority of secondary schools.

Choirs and Choruses. The terms *choir* and *chorus* are used interchangeably by many authors and directors to denote large groups of mixed voices. Originally a body of church singers was called a choir as opposed to a group singing secular music. Because school groups sing both sacred and secular music this differentiation has lost its significance.

Some music educators believe that it is wise to have separate groups for boys and girls at the junior high school level, usually called glee clubs, and unite them forming a choir or chorus only for special occasions. The mixed chorus or choir is favored generally for senior high school students if only one vocal group is to be scheduled. All types should be maintained whenever the size of the student body permits.

The term *a cappella* means literally 'for the choir of a chapel' and an a cappella choir literally is one formed for the singing of unaccompanied sacred music. Because it is desirable to use both accompanied and unaccompanied literature with either sacred or secular origin and texts, some directors use the term *a cappella choir* to designate a more highly selected group of singers. This being the case, the choir approaches a club or school organization while the chorus is thought of more as a regular school class. This should not minimize in any way the importance of the group designated as a chorus. The seating arrangements, voice classifications, and general techniques of instruction will be the same with perhaps the only differentiation being one of difficulty of material used.
59 to 61.)

Voice Classification

The same voice testing procedure as outlined in Chapter X may be followed for all unchanged voices. The changed voices will begin their testing exercises on "G" located in the fourth space bass clef, and follow the same form used for unchanged voices. (See pages

EXERCISE I.

EXERCISE II.

EXERCISE III.

EXERCISE IV.

The girls' voices may be classified as:

1. First soprano, with a range from "C", line below the staff to "G" or "A" above the staff. The quality must be clear, light and unpinched, resembling a flute.
2. Second soprano, with a range from "C", line below the staff, to "E" in the fourth space. The quality is fundamentally soprano, but not quite as brilliant as a first soprano.
3. First alto, with a range from "G" in the third space below the staff to "C" in the third space. The quality will be mezzo with a developed lower range.
4. Second alto, with a range from "G" in the third added space below the staff to "G" on the second line, with a broad contralto quality.

The boys' voices may be classified as:

1. Unchanged voices
    a. First soprano, same as girls' voices
    b. Second soprano, same as girls' voices
    c. First alto, same as girls' voices
    d. Second alto, same as girls' voices
    e. Alto-tenor, a name applied to an unchanged voice that is able to meet the requirements of the regular changed tenor. An alto-tenor may be assigned to sing either an alto or a tenor part.
2. Changed voices
    a. First tenor, light quality corresponding to the soprano in girls' voices. The range is from "G" on the second line treble clef to "E" in the third space bass clef.
    b. Second tenor, light and clear in quality but range from "E", first line treble clef to "E" in the third space bass clef.
    c. Baritone, heavier quality tending to broaden in lower tones. The range is approximately the same as the second tenor, the chief difference being one of quality.
    d. Bass, the quality is full and open with a range from "G" on the first line bass clef to "C" on the first added line above the bass staff.

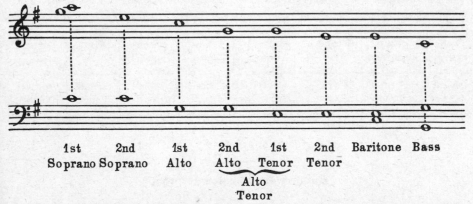

It is impossible to predict what kind of voice combination a test will reveal. One cannot say that all seventh grades shall sing three-part music for unchanged voices or any other voice combination. A junior high school chorus may test out in any of the following voice combinations.

1. S-S-A (first soprano, second soprano, alto)
2. S-A-B (soprano, alto, baritone)
3. S-A-T-B (soprano, alto, tenor, bass or baritone)

A senior high school chorus or choir may test out in any of the following voice combinations.

1. S-A-B (same as 2 above)
2. S-A-T-B (same as 3 above)
3. S-S-A-T-B (first soprano, second soprano, alto, tenor, baritone or bass)
4. S-S-A-A-T-T-B-B (first and second voices in all four parts)

Seating Arrangements

The seating of the group as well as the material used will depend upon the voice combination, and the details of the seating will depend upon the number singing each part, the size and shape of the room etc. The following seating plans are acceptable.

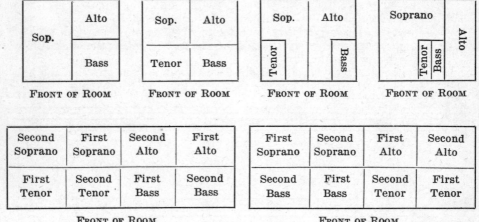

Second Soprano	First Soprano	Second Alto	First Alto
First Tenor	Second Tenor	First Bass	Second Bass

FRONT OF ROOM

First Soprano	Second Soprano	First Alto	Second Alto
Second Bass	First Bass	Second Tenor	First Tenor

FRONT OF ROOM

Balance in Selected Groups

Power and quality as well as the number of students assigned to each part need to be considered in any decision concerning balance. The total size of any selected choir will depend largely upon the number of available first tenors because the other voice parts will need to balance with the high male voices. After the membership

112

has been selected the individuals will need guidance and practice in adjusting their singing so as to improve and maintain a beauty of balance within the section as well as within the entire group. It should be noted in the following distribution that the female voices approximate three-fifths of the group and that the largest numbers are in the first-soprano and second-bass parts.

For a choir of thirty-five voices

12 sopranos		9 altos		5 tenors		9 Bass	
7 first sopranos	5 second sopranos	4 first altos	5 second altos	3 first tenors	2 second tenors	3 first bass	6 second bass

For a choir of sixty voices.

20 sopranos		16 altos		10 tenors		14 Bass	
12 first sopranos	8 second sopranos	7 first altos	9 second altos	4 first tenors	6 second tenors	6 first bass	8 second bass

Items for Selective Consideration

Records should be made at the time of try-out for selective groups for future reference as well as for immediate use. The following list of data will prove helpful in choosing members for any selected group.

Name_____ School or Home Room Number_____ Date_____
Address_____ Telephone Number_____
Previous Choral Experience_____
_____ Grade_____

1. Range_____
2. Quality_____
3. Size of Tone_____
4. Pitch Accuracy_____
5. Rhythmic Accuracy_____
6. Flexibility_____

7. Tremolo_____
8. Personality_____
9. Other Musical Interests_____
10. Scholarship_____
11. Classification Assignment_____
12. Remarks_____

Glee Clubs. The word *glee* is derived from the Anglo-Saxon word *gligg,* meaning simply *music.* Traditionally it had the following characteristics, (a) unaccompanied, (b) for male voices, and (c) harmonic rather than contrapuntal in style. In the eighteenth century the glee and the catch were intermingled. Today the name glee club is used for either boys' or girls' singing groups and the music used is usually in close harmony and of a light entertainment nature.

Boys' glee clubs flourish especially well at the junior high school level and are popular with students and audiences. Unchanged, changing, and changed voices may be used. The following seating or standing order will assist in the blending of voices for newly organized groups of immature boy singers.

1. First tenor, baritone, bass, second tenor
2. Second soprano, alto-tenor, bass, alto

Girls' glee clubs are one of the easiest performing groups to organize. The material should be largely accompanied and written in three parts due to the lack of real second-alto voices at this age. Care will need to be taken to have the music worthwhile and beautiful. The following seating or standing order is suggested.

1. Second soprano, first soprano, alto
2. First soprano, second soprano, alto

Small Vocal Ensembles. This is one of the most rewarding types of vocal organizations because it develops leadership and leavens the choirs and choruses. Because of the small number of students involved, they can be of great service to both school and community. While situations may arise which make it advisable to select a small ensemble from members of a larger choral group to perform at a special occasion, this should be the exception. Small ensembles should be a music unit organized at the beginning of the school term, have try-outs, regular rehearsals, and a definite plan if a real feeling for ensemble singing is to be developed.

The small ensemble affords opportunity for students of superior ability to sing the lovely material available for madrigal groups, quartets and double-quartets, trios and double-trios, etc. Many groups of varying levels of artistic musical performance should be organized and they may be initiated by faculty or at student suggestion. Regardless of the origin or type of ensemble they should merit the approval, helpful interest, and guidance of the secondary vocal music teacher provided they serve for educational, musical, and social development.

It has been found advisable with young singers to use at least two voices on each part for assurance and tone quality. For example, eight voices singing two on a part would constitute a double-quartet and is usually more effective than the same number constituting an octet with one voice for each part. In the junior high school the usual practice is to use at least three students for each part forming triple-trios and triple-quartets.

Voice Class. This course provides instruction in the correct use of the singing voice by giving group and individual help to the more talented. Only those with adequate training and experience in voice work should teach voice classes. This would assume a knowledge of generally accepted standards of good tone production and performance as well as techniques for achieving these standards.

While some schools allow thirty students to enroll in one voice class, it is considered that better work can be done with groups of fifteen to twenty. Some schools organize separate classes for boys and girls, others have them working separately on individually suitable material but meeting together in the same class. The reasons advanced for mixed voice classes are, (a) vocal fundamentals such

114

as breath, diction, posture, etc., are common to all voices, and (b) the seeming preference of the students.

Some guidance is desirable in the selection of solo material and can be accomplished easily by adequate lists of acceptable songs classified according to ballads, sacred songs, operatic and oratorio arias, classic, romantic, etc., from which students may choose. Duets and selections for small ensembles should be included. It is well to avoid overly sentimental songs. Unless the teacher is capable of presenting songs with words in a foreign language both as to correct pronunciation and thought content, only songs in English should be used. With such a vast amount of superior literature available there is no logical reason for the use of any selection which could be questioned. Folios, books of song collections, and voice class technique books have been published which serve a splendid purpose.

Some Selected Vocal Techniques

While much should be left to the discretion and desires of the well trained director of secondary school vocal music groups, a few selected general techniques may serve as guides.

Posture. Proper posture for singing is simply to place the entire body so that the singing apparatus can function to the best advantage. This would mean the maintenance of an erect body position, whether standing or sitting. The head should be held high as though pushing up with the top of the head which will place the chin at almost right angles but the head should not have a rigid set. The shoulders will be relaxed and quiet with the chest comfortably high and the abdomen held in slightly. In standing there should be a comfortably balanced stance, and in sitting, the weight of the trunk should be supported by the hips with the back of the body not supported by the back of the chair. This posture assures free action of the muscles used in breathing. The expression of 'feeling tall' used with elementary children is effective also with secondary school students in achieving desirable posture for singing.

Diction. Correct pronunciation and clear enunciation result in a diction which enhances the over-all beauty of vocal presentation and enables the listener to understand the text. Continual stress should be given to the fact that music is a communicative art and even though words are wedded to tone, they must be understood.

Some unique and startling techniques for achieving superb diction have been used by some individuals with varying degrees of success. However, in the hands of others these same techniques have been rather disastrous. For example, the use of exaggerated lip movements, which is a common technique, may lead to distortion if used

115

to excess; the stressing of the first syllable of a word detracts from the final syllable of the preceding word and may tend to upset the natural rhythmic flow; likewise where vowels are unduly stressed the effectiveness of the consonants suffer. It would seem wise, therefore, to use a number of different techniques chosen as the situation arises but not to use any one technique to the exclusion of all others.

Songs with words which must be sung at a rapid tempo such as *"Marianina"*, an Italian folk song, *"The Hopak"*, a Russian folk song, or *"Deck the Halls"*, an old Welsh air, will aid in attaining free action of the tongue, lips, jaw and soft palate. Students and director should be alert continually in order to avoid any change in vowel form while singing a sustained tone and to avoid any interference with the vowel form by consonants.

The use of tape or wire recording devices which permit immediate play back enables the individual or group to 'hear themselves as others hear them', and will validate the use of techniques which have been effective in achieving the desired articulation.

Tone Quality and Production. Various words have been used to describe an acceptable tone quality but the ideal approach is through demonstration so that the student may hear patterns and thus get a conception almost impossible by word description. These demonstrations may be made by the teacher, selected students, artists in concert or on radio and television, as well as recordings. In some ways a proper tone quality is like a pungent odor, once it is identified it is not easily forgotten.

It is important that the singing tones have vitality whether being used pianissimo or fortissimo. This vitality will result from an expression of the emotional content of the text in combination with a 'mental image' of good tone quality. This acceptable tone is the result of coordination of several physical factors but usually it is unwise with immature and inexperienced singers to isolate and over-stress any one factor from the physiological aspect.

Some Effective Exercises

Exercises should be used when they are needed to improve a specific situation rather than as a routine class procedure. Often all that is necessary is to isolate the tonal pattern or phrase from the song being studied and use it for exercise purposes. The following exercises are only suggestive.

1. Scales, tetrachords, arpeggios and triads; sustained and staccato; ascending and descending; using vowels, diphthongs, and syllables such as:
   a. Open vowels—äh (father), ō (row), o͞o (boot), e͞e (feet)

b. Diphthongs — i (ä-ēē—fine), ā (ā-ēē—day), oy (aw-ēē—joy), ou (ä-ōō—about), ew (ēē-ōō—few)

c. Syllables. By the addition of l, m, n, p, b, f, and g, to the open vowel and diphtong sounds, countless helpful syllables may be devised.

2. The following cadences may be used as sustained chords or in slow progression while listening to the tone quality, intonation, and balance of parts.

a. SSA

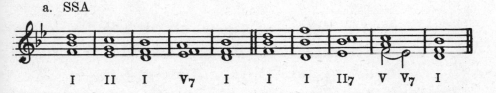

I   II   I   V₇   I   I   I   II₇   V   V₇   I

b. SAB

I   V₇   V   I   I   IV   II₆   I⁶₄   V   I

c. SATB

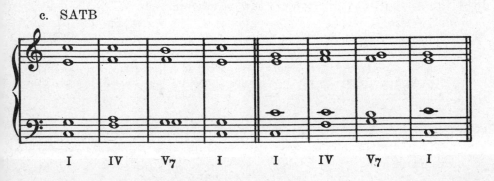

I   IV   V₇   I   I   IV   V₇   I

117

d. SSAATTBB

I IV II₇ V₇ I I VI III VI II₇ V₇ I

Breathing While Singing. If the correct posture is assumed, breathing while singing will be normal and adequate. Breath is basic to artistic singing and should be considered from two angles, namely: (a) how to have adequate breath, and (b) when to inhale.

For most school singing it is advisable to approach the 'how' of adequate breath by the use of fairly long phrases from the song literature being studied. Abstract breathing exercises apart from tone production have proved of little or doubtful value. It is as undesirable to have the lungs filled too full of air as it is to completely exhaust the supply before reaching the end of a phrase. This breath balance or adequacy is acquired by rehearsal and experience.

The 'where' of taking a breath is controlled largely by the text of the material sung. Some composers indicate where they intend breaths to be taken by the use of an apostrophe (') above the staff. Rests in the music are unmistakable as opportunities for inhalations. A close scrutiny of the text in conjunction with the music will show where the tone and word may be stopped ideally for a replenishment of breath without disturbing the rhythmic flow of the music. In some instances it may not be necessary or desirable to use every opportunity afforded. It is important to remember the following.

1. A breath should not be taken between the syllables of a word, between a word and its modifier, nor between a phrase and the word it modifies.
2. The rhythmic flow of the music must not be broken for breath taking. If necessary, the time for a catch breath should be taken from the departure tone and not from the attacked tone.
3. Breath should be conserved during the first half of the phrase. It is a common fault to expend more breath than is necessary on the first few tones and then not have sufficient breath for an effective completion of the phrase.

4. Where the effectiveness of an impossibly long phrase demands that it be unbroken by simultaneous inhalation by the entire group, certain individuals may be charged with taking a breath at unorthodox times to assure an uninterrupted flow of the tone.

Interpretation. The printed music page comes to life and beauty through the interpretation given it by the director and performers. This assumes that the director has knowledge of the style unique to numerous composers as well as that of the various periods of choral composition.

The study of any vocal number should begin with an over-all concept of what it is trying to say and in what manner. This may be accomplished by a rapid reading of the text and a quick glance at the music to see how it reinforces the text, and to give information about key, rhythm, etc. If discussion is necessary for clarification, it should be kept at a minimum.

Sudden changes of dynamics and tempo should be studiously avoided unless justification is found in the selection as this savors of exhibitionism. Variation is desirable within a selection, between selections, and even at repeated presentations of the same selection. However, as desirable as variation in interpretation often is, it should always be in good taste and never be distortion.

The subtleties of interpretation are to be found in two areas, (a) the rhythmic flow of the music which should carry throughout the entire number without unwarranted interruption, and (b) due attention to the phrase line so that it is a well rounded unit. This is sometimes called 'phrase rise and fall'.

Materials. The vocal material used with secondary school groups will be in the form of (a) basic music textbooks which are the upper books of an adopted series, (b) collections, chosen on a basis of voice combination, or (c) octavo selections. Each have distinct advantages and music in all forms should be available.

One of the most serious errors committed by directors of vocal music is their insistence on 'fitting the voices to the music' instead of 'fitting the music to the voices'. It is difficult to understand why an intelligent music teacher who has few low-bass or high-tenor voices in his chorus or choir, will labor to perform music in eight parts when wisdom cries for four-part material which is within the range and ability of the students who constitute the group.

As the average untrained voice has quite a limited range in which it can be used with good quality and with safety, care must be taken that music selected is within the range of the voices in all sections. It should be remembered that the welfare of the individual voice is more important than ambition on the part of the director or even the balance of parts within an elective singing group.

Standard classic and contemporary selections as well as anthems, folk songs, etc., should be used in order to give adequate repertoire balance. The technical aspects should be of progressive difficulty to provide opportunity for development. Material to be used on special days and events should be selected well in advance so as to allow for preparation during regular class time.

The final choice of material will be determined by the voice combination and ability present in the specific group, the purpose for which the material is to be used, and the training and preference of the teacher in charge.

Period vs. Grade Level Organization. Due to the way class schedules are made for secondary schools, it may be found wise to have a large mixed choral group organized on a period basis which is open to all students regardless of grade, as opposed to a chorus scheduled so that it is comprised of only those in a single grade. This would result, for example, in what might be called a Third Period Chorus instead of an Eleventh Grade Chorus. As a general practice, the grade type of organization is followed in the junior high school and the period type used in the senior high school. It is recognized that there are values unique to each type of organization and these should be capitalized.

Class or Rehearsal Routine. After the material has been carefully selected and prepared by the teacher *before* the scheduled time for the class to meet, a suggested simple routine for saving time and techniques for getting things done may be helpful. Item I, below, should take only a very short time, item II should have the major portion of the rehearsal period, while item III should be quite brief.

I. Preliminary
   a. Attendance
   b. The singing of a familiar song
   c. Exercises (if needed)

II. New Work
   a. Song analysis (key, tempo, mood, etc.)
   b. Procedure
      1. Sing clear through with words unless the song falls apart. Rehearse and clear up one thing at a time such as pitch, rhythm, enunciation, etc. Develop an evaluating attitude.
      2. Isolate difficulties (where the song falls apart); if it is necessary to take the parts separately, always start with the lowest parts. Don't use the piano to feed the parts to the extent that it becomes a necessary prop.
      3. If the piano is an integral part of the selection it should be used. Do not hesitate to take it away to make the errors more apparent.

4. Don't drive on one selection until all are exhausted. Better have several selections in preparation.

III. Review
   a. Always sing some finished material at the close of the class. This should be in the nature of public performance rather than pure recreation.
   b. The students as well as the director must have a feeling of accomplishment and knowledge of progress at the end of each class or rehearsal.

Conclusion. As students eagerly participate in choral activities which challenge their ability and give them inner satisfactions, their pleasure in accomplishment reflects on, and is absorbed by the vocal music teacher, who, with patient understanding has guided them forward in an art which will ever enrich their experiences.

The educational, musical, and social development which can be achieved through singing together is an integral part of our democratic way of life.

INSTRUMENTAL MUSIC IN SECONDARY SCHOOLS

A recent survey found that sixty-eight percent of secondary school instrumental players actually started their playing in the elementary grades.* It would follow then that the size of secondary school instrumental organizations and the beginning level of instrumental performance will depend largely upon the instrumental program which has been carried on in the elementary schools. And further, it would behoove junior and senior high school instrumental directors to be interested in and informed about what is taking place in the elementary schools from which his players come. (See Chapter V.)

While in many instances these instrumental groups, whether large or small, serve the student chiefly in the areas of general and educational development, their major musical purpose consists of, (a) opportunity for musical experience and technical improvement, (b) contact with repertoire, (c) raising standards of appreciation, (d) service to school and community, and (e) giving a life enrichment.

This chapter will be concerned with orchestras, bands, small ensembles, instrumental technique classes, and some selected teaching suggestions.

Orchestra. In the early Greek theater the space situated between the auditorium and the stage was reserved for the dancing chorus and the instrumentalists. The word *orchestra* is derived from the Greek and means literally 'dancing place'. Gradually the dancers were moved to the stage and the musicians occupied the orchestra area and thus the assemblage of instrumentalists became known as an orchestra. The use of instruments in combination is probably as old as the instruments themselves and the development of the orchestra as it is known today is closely allied with certain composers who wrote for ever enlarged and diversified groups of instrumentalists.

School systems where the teaching of string instruments is begun in the lower grades will have no difficulty in developing a secondary school orchestra which can provide vital musical experience. It is desirable that all members of the orchestra and especially the string

*Study by L. Bruce Jones, Baton Rouge, Louisiana.

players, continue with class or private lessons during the secondary school years.

An effective orchestra is the result of long-range planning but this should not deter an instrumental director from gathering together available string players, adding to them the other requisite instruments when possible and making a start on the developmental process.

Instrumentation

An orchestra group may have its beginning with a small ensemble of a piano and two or three other instruments. The following instrumentation will indicate typical balance.

Schools of 100 or less Enrolment	Average Junior High School Minimum	Average Senior High School Minimum
4-6 violins	8-10 violins	10 violins
1-2 cellos	2-3 cellos	2 violas
1 bass	1-2 basses	2 cellos
1 flute	2 flutes	2 basses
2 clarinets	2 clarinets	2 flutes
2 trumpets	2 horns	1 oboe
1 trombone	2 trumpets	2 clarinets
1 percussion	1 trombone	1 bassoon
1 piano	1 tuba	2 horns
	2 percussion	2 trumpets
	1 piano	1 trombone
		2 percussion
		1 piano

Ideal Junior or Senior High School	Standard Symphony Orchestra
10-16 first violins	16-20 first violins
8-14 second violins	14-18 second violins
6-12 violas	10-12 violas
5-10 cellos	8-10 cellos
4-8 basses	8-10 basses
1 harp	2-3 flutes (one to double on piccolo)
2-4 flutes	2-3 oboes (one to double English horn)
2-3 oboes	2-4 Clarinets
2-4 clarinets	2-3 bassoons
2-3 bassoons	4-6 French horns
4-6 horns	2-4 trumpets
2-4 trumpets	3 trombones
3 trombones	1 tuba
1 tuba	4 percussion (one tympani, 3 drums)
1 tympani	1-2 harps
3 percussion	

Band. The word band originates from the Italian *banda,* meaning a group of brass and percussion players but the Harvard Dictionary of Music defines a band as an orchestral group composed principally of wind instruments.

The chief differentiation between a band and an orchestra on a basis of instruments represented, is that while both are classed as large ensembles, the wind instruments comprise the backbone of the band, and string instruments serve this purpose for an orchestra. A further differentiation will be noted in the type of music performed as this is in accordance with the range, tone color, etc. of the instruments which comprise the group.

There are various names applied to bands, such as symphonic, concert, marching, dance, etc., depending on the kind of music used, the size of the organization, or the purpose it serves.

Since about 1920, the band as a school music activity has developed from an extra-curricular, after-school affair to one of the most prominent of secondary school music organizations. It has become musically dignified and has earned a place of recognition along with that of the orchestra because it affords unique development and service. Some of this interest and development was engendered by the many service bands which participated in World War I.

It should be remembered that an orchestra has need for a comparatively few wind instruments in proportion to the membership and the band affords opportunity for many wind instrument players.

Instrumentation

It is possible for only fifteen players to constitute an aggregation of band instruments which can play creditably. Many schools with a total population of one-hundred or less produce bands of at least twenty-four players. The following instrumentation will aid in attaining comparative balance.

Minimum For Any Band	Schools of 100 or less Enrolment
1 piccolo (to double on flute)	1 flute (piccolo)
3 clarinets	6 Bb clarinets
1 Eb saxaphone	1 alto sax
4 Bb cornets	1 tenor sax
2 horns or melophones	6 cornets or trumpets
1 Bb baritone	2 horns (alto or French)
2 trombones	2 trombones
1 bass	1 baritone
(Percussion as available)	1 tuba
	3 percussion

2 flutes (piccolo)
12 Bb clarinets
2 alto sax
1 tenor sax
4 cornets
2 trumpets
3 Eb alto horns
3 trombones
1 baritone
3 tubas
3 percussion

3 flutes (piccolo)
1 oboe
16 Bb clarinets
1 alto clarinet
1 bass clarinet
1 bassoon
2 alto sax
1 tenor sax
6 cornets
2 trumpets
4 Eb or F horns
4 or 5 trombones
2 baritones
4 tubas
3 percussion

Ideal
Junior or Senior
High School

5 flutes (one to double on piccolo)
2 Eb clarinets
24 Bb clarinets (or more)
2 alto clarinets
2 bass clarinets
2 oboes (or more, one to double on
   English horn)
2 bassons (or more)
5 saxophones
4 Bb cornets (or more)
4 Bb trumpets (or more)
4-8 French horns
4-6 trombones
2-4 baritones
2 E tubas
4 BBb flat tubas
2 string basses
1 harp
1 tympani
3 other percussion

Standard
Symphonic
Band

3 flutes (piccolo)
2 oboes
24 Bb clarinets
1 Eb clarinet
2 alto clarinets
2 bass clarinets
2 bassoons
2 alto sax
1 tenor sax
1 baritone sax
8 cornets
2 trumpets
4 F horns
5 trombones
2 baritones
6 tubas
1 tympani
3 percussion

Marching or Parade Band

While the purpose of a marching band is limited and of a utility nature, it usually accomplishes two important ends, namely, (a) demonstrates cooperation with the athletic department, and (b) attracts attention of the community to the entire music program offered at the school.

Some band directors recommend that all material to be used on parade should be memorized by the players. This is especially true of an inexperienced group. Considerable field work will need to be done before attempting any public appearance and the following techniques will need to be mastered before attempting special or pictorial maneuvers.*

1. Required Movements:
   a. Forward March
   b. Halt
   c. Column Right
   d. Column Left
   e. Countermarch
   f. Diminish Front
   g. Increase Front
   h. Choice of Right Oblique, Left Oblique, Column Half Right, or Column Half Left
   i. Start Playing and Cease Playing
2. Playing. Volume; balance, rhythm, selection.
3. Cadence. Metronome tempo; regularity, suitability to style of marching.
4. Carriage. Personal bearing; position of instruments; length and manner of step.
5. Alignment. Straightness of ranks; straightness of files; uniformity of interval; uniformity of distance.
6. Precision. Uniformity of action; military character of movement.
7. Inspection. Condition of uniform; condition of instrument.
8. Discipline. Individual; organization.

The diagram for marching band formation given below is used by many schools and is considered basic for a small band. Adaptations

Forward

↑

| DRUM MAJOR |

4th File	3rd File	2nd File	1st File	
E flat Tuba	2nd Trombone	1st Trombone	BB flat Tuba	1st Rank (platoon)
Alto Saxophone	2nd Alto	1st Alto	Baritone	2nd Rank
3rd Trumpet	2nd Trumpet	1st Trumpet	Solo Trumpet	3rd Rank
Solo Clarinet	1st Clarinet	2nd Clarinet	Piccolo	4th Rank
Bass Drum	Asst. Solo Trumpet	Cymbals	Snare Drum	5th Rank

| CONDUCTOR |

*Judges' Marching Comment Sheet. National School Band Association.

126

will be necessary to accommodate the instrumentation of the individual school band and the number of players. In any adaptation it should be remembered that it is very important to place solo instruments, tubas, and drums so that they can be heard by all players.

Small Instrumental Ensembles. The general advantages and benefits from small ensemble participation which were indicated for vocal ensembles apply equally as well to instrumental ensembles. (See page 114.) The vast literature of chamber music can be brought to life only by combinations of players for which this music was written.

The possible combinations are many and extend from duets, requiring two players, to concerto grossos calling for duplicated string quartets with two to five solo wind instruments. They may be composed of instruments from one family, as string trios, string quartets, etc., or combinations from different families.

Small instrumental ensembles should be organized around the instruments which are available and no school is too small to have several. The usual ensembles found in secondary schools are:
1. String trio; piano, violin, 'cello
2. String quartet; 1st violin, 2nd violin, viola, 'cello
3. Brass quartet; 1st trumpet, 2nd trumpet, trombone or horn, bass
4. Brass sextet; 1st trumpet, 2nd trumpet, French horn, trombone, baritone, tuba
5. Woodwind quintet; flute, oboe, clarinet, French horn, bassoon

Instrumental Technique Classes. An instrumental technique class may be described as a group of pupils having approximately the same level of playing proficiency on their respective instruments, meeting regularly with an instructor in order to acquire greater technique for playing and broader musical development.

These classes are supplementary to the larger performing instrumental groups and their existance can be justified from the angle of musical progress, educational values, and economy of time and money.

Class Grouping

The kinds of instruments which can be taught together with profit to all concerned has undergone considerable experimentation. The common groupings usually used are:
(1) *Single Instrument.* The advantages of this grouping are self-evident. It is largely used by those who believe in instrumental classes on three basic instruments, namely: cornet, clarinet, and violin. This has proven successful when adequate provision is made

for change-over to other instruments which are less common but which are in the same instrument family.

(2) *Same Instrument Family.* This grouping would call for string, woodwind, brass, and percussion classes. While the number of problems common to all students will be less than in the single instrument grouping, this has the advantage of economy of time for the teacher, availability of varied instrumental instruction, and eliminates change-over.

(3) *All Instruments.* Where any and all kinds of instruments are included in one class it is important to try to group according to playing ability. This would result in beginning, intermediate, and advanced technique classes. The progress will be slower than either of the above groupings on account of the many technical problems, the advantages should be capitalized whenever this is the only solution possible in the local situation.

The Teacher

The teacher of instrumental technique classes should be an expert performer on at least one instrument and have adequate knowledge of all other instruments. In addition he must be an understanding music educator.

While technical improvement will be an outcome of all good band and orchestra rehearsals, these rehearsals should not be considered as class lessons in instrumental technique. The membership in a technique class should not terminate when the student is admitted to a larger playing group.

SUGGESTIONS FOR SELECTED AREAS

Music educators interested primarily in instrumental music activities will find considerable help in the following suggestions, but other bibliography should be consulted for additional sources of assistance.

Membership. The basis for membership in any band or orchestra will depend upon the number of available and interested players. It will vary from small schools where all who elect to participate are accepted, to highly organized competition for membership. The quality of the musical performance will be affected by the degree of selectivity.

The technical ability of the individual player, including sight reading, is considered by some to be the most desirable asset in selecting a player. It has been demonstrated that other factors such as co-operation, dependability, and scholarship are very important.

Rehearsal and Class Schedule. The degree of excellency of performance of any instrumental group is in direct proportion to the amount of time devoted to well-planned rehearsal. General rehearsals should meet during school time and are usually scheduled as a regular class. Two periods of forty-five minutes in length per week is considered a bare minimum but many schools provide for one rehearsal period each day. General rehearsals are concerned primarily with the perfecting of the group as an ensemble. The specific items which need technical improvement should be taken care of in sectional rehearsals.

During sectional rehearsals individual attention can be given to each player thus enhancing his progress and saving time at the general meetings. With guidance from the director, section leaders or assistants may conduct the sectional rehearsal.

All rehearsals, whether general or sectional, require certain well organized routines which will minimize confusion and develop personal responsibility in each student. These routines will involve taking attendance, tuning of the instrument, distribution and collection of music, proper location of racks and chairs, and items in connection with dismissal.

Instrument Substitution. Many band instructors find they have an over supply of players on certain instruments and lack players of other important instruments. It is recognized that no substitution can supply the tone quality of the original instrument indicated by the composer, however, certain balance and harmonic completeness can be achieved by intelligent use of substitution. The following exchanges are possible with a minimum musical loss.

PART	MAY BE TAKEN BY
Piccolo	Flute, E♭ Clarinet
Flute	Clarinets (1st and 2nd)
Oboe	Muted Trumpets, Clarinets
E♭ Clarinet	Flute
Alto Clarinet	Saxophone (Alto or Tenor)
Bass Clarinet	Tenor Saxophone, Bassoon
Bassoon	Baritone, Tenor or Baritone Saxophone
Soprano Saxophone	Solo Cornet
Alto Saxophone	First Cornet, Baritone
Tenor Saxophone	Trombone, Baritone
Baritone Saxophone	Tuba
Bass Saxophone	Tuba
Trumpet	Cornet
Cornet	Trumpet
Fluegelhorn	Cornet
E♭ Alto (3rd and 4th)	Trombone, Alto Saxophone
French Horn	Alto or Tenor Saxophone, Trombone
Baritone	Tenor Saxophone, Trombone, Alto or Bass Clarinet
Trombone	Baritone
Tuba	Baritone or Bass Saxophone

Playing Range of Instruments. In order to write or make arrangements for orchestral and band instruments it is necessary to have clearly in mind the complete playing range of each instrument. The following illustrations show the *actual* pitch and range grouped according to family. In writing music to be played by inexperienced players, the use of the extreme limits of the instrument should be avoided as the middle tones or practical playing range will be in better tune and call for less physical strain.

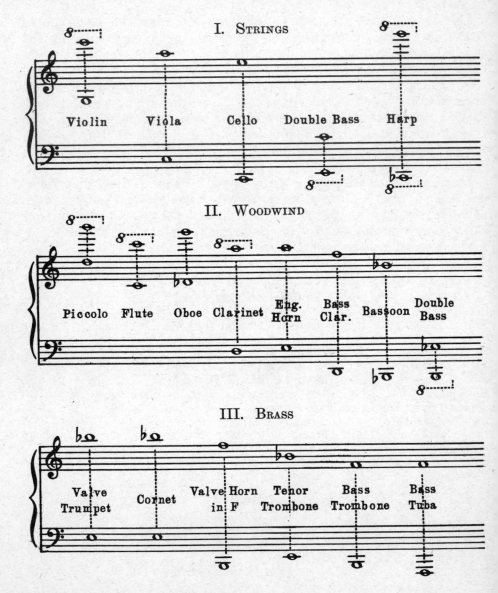

Transposition. A knowledge of the basic principles of transposition is essential for all instrumentalists. A few fundamentals to remember are:

1. The key name of each instrument indicates the resultant pitch sounded when the player reads the written tone "C". For example: the B♭ clarinet sounds B♭ when reading the written "C".
2. Instruments built in "C" sound the exact pitch written except the C Tenor Saxophone which sounds an octave below that written.
3. Items 1 and 2 above do not hold true for instruments using the bass clef. They always sound the pitch of the tone as written.

The following is a list of instruments with a tone indicated as written and as heard.

Instrument	As Written	As Heard
Violin, C Flute, Oboe		
C Tenor (Melody) Saxophone		
D♭ Piccolo		
E♭ Clarinet		
Viola		
B♭ Clarinet, B♭ Soprano Saxophone, B♭ Cornet (Trumpet)		
B♭ Baritone, B♭ Tenor Saxophone, B♭ Bass Clarinet		

Instrument	As Written	As Heard

Eb Alto Saxophone
Eb Fr. Horn (Melophone)
Eb Alto Clarinet

Eb Baritone Saxophone

Bb Bass Saxophone

Cello
Bassoon
Euphonium
Eb and BBb Basses

String Bass

School Owned Instruments. It is understandable that students and parents are interested primarily in the purchase of solo instruments and especially those in the soprano range. It is just as important for schools to supply needed musical instruments as any other laboratory equipment, however, other sources such as Service Clubs, Federated Music Clubs, and Parent Teacher Associations, often will assist where the school is not financially able. While it is not an ideal procedure, the music groups sometimes raise money for the purchase of needed instruments by giving concerts and entertainments.

The usual instruments supplied by schools are string basses, violas, 'cellos, tubas, French horns, oboes, bassoons, bass clarinets, English horns, tympani, and bass drums. A rental fee may be charged for the use of school owned instruments which will be sufficient to keep the instrument and case in repair.

It is never economy to purchase a cheap or inferior instrument but better grade second-hand instruments in good condition may serve very adequately.

Balance. The term balance as applied to large instrumental music groups has two aspects to be considered, (a) adequate representation of instruments in all sections, and (b) artistic balance in production. In large schools efficient players usually are available for all instruments and only try-outs to select the most proficient are necessary. However, most school instrumental directors are faced with the problem of unbalance in both numbers and tone color. It is a waste

132

of time and energy to regret the existance of the problem or worse still, to delay starting an organization until acceptable balance is present. The thing to do is to start with what is available and work towards an ideal situation.

Seating Arrangements. The seating arrangement of a band or orchestra should be such as to place the players so that each one may see the director and also hear distinctly the other parts most necessary to assist his own playing. The plan also should be such that the ensemble of sound (melody, rhythm and harmony), will reach the audience most effectively.

The details of the position of players will depend upon, (a) the size and shape of the floor space used, (b) the absence or presence of elevations, (c) the size of the entire room, and (d) the personal preference of the director. If at all possible the same seating arrangement should be maintained for both rehearsal and performance. It is especially important at rehearsals that sufficient space be allowed so that the director may have ready access to any member of the group in order to give special directions and assistance.

The following seating plans are considered very desirable but there should be no hesitancy to make adjustments which will be advantageous.

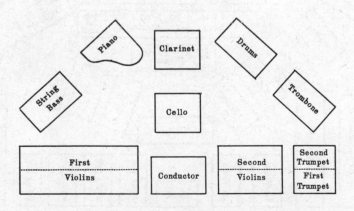

I. SMALL ORCHESTRA USING PIANO

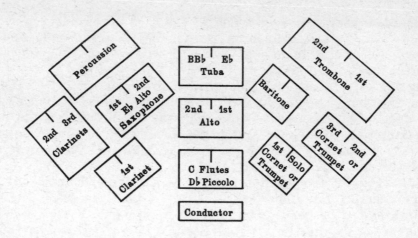

II. SMALL BAND

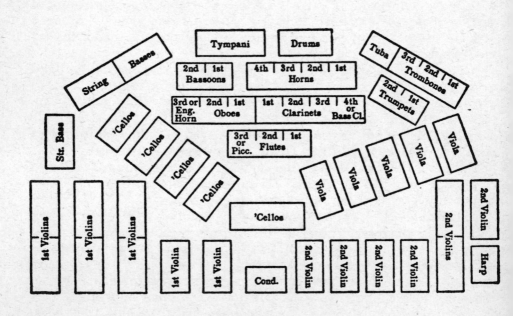

III. SYMPHONY ORCHESTRA

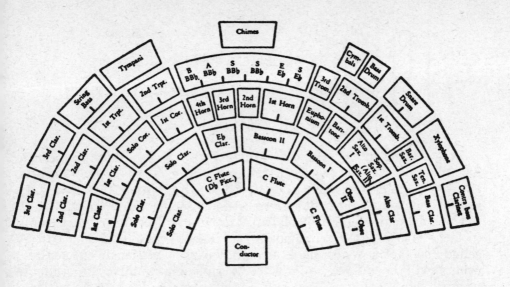

IV. Symphonic Band

Materials. There has been a tremendous increase recently in instrumental publications for school use. Publishers are cooperating with music educators in order to make available school editions of worthy music so arranged that the musical value is not destroyed and yet are within the technical ability of secondary school instrumentalists.

It is wisdom to select music which gives all sections of the band or orchestra an opportunity to play and thereby improve. There are obvious reasons why music should be avoided which have prominent parts for instruments which are not available or where suitable substitutions cannot be made. Selections used in public performance should be restricted to those which can be played artistically.

The care and handling of the instrumental music library should be in the hands of an elected or appointed librarian who will be responsible for distribution, collection and repair.

Conclusion. The reward for careful planning and sincere work with young players of musical instruments is both immediate and far reaching. It carries satisfaction and pleasure because some few will continue to progress until they become professional performers and fill places of importance in major symphonies, others will enrich the home and community. All will have a unique appreciation of the intricacies of instrumental music when heard because they have a basis, not only for critical evaluation, but for real inner satisfaction.

19

OTHER MUSIC CLASSES AND ACTIVITIES

In addition to the General Music Class and performing music organizations as discussed in the preceding three chapters, there are other music classes and activities with which the secondary school music teacher will be concerned. Some are common to all junior and senior high schools while others will be encountered only in large consolidated or metropolitan school systems. Some will be scheduled each school term as a regular part of the music curriculum, others will be offered only when a sufficient number of students request the offering. Some will be extra-curricular and be entirely student organized and controlled.

Music Classes

Music Reading. This should be an elective course directed toward improving the quality and speed of the reading at first sight of musical scores. Music reading is a skill and therefore this class will consist of purposeful drill and exercise, the elimination of faulty practices, and the establishment of helpful music reading habits. Any student who contemplates music as a vocation should be very sure that he has a mastery of this skill. In most instances this is accomplished in the various music classes but when sufficient students need specific assistance in reading the printed music page, it is advantageous to offer such a course.

Music History and Appreciation. In far too many secondary schools the only contact with music history and music appreciation which students have is that which is given them incidentally by teachers of performing music groups.

When a course is scheduled, the trend is to combine courses in history of music, which is basically academic, with music appreciation, which has laboratory implications. It has been found that each enhances the other very effectively.

The course content may be organized in various ways such as in chronological historical order, in reverse-chronological order, or by topical units based upon epochs or style. Use of illustrative music and material is highly desirable.

136

Music Theory. It is a common belief that theoretical items should be explained whenever they are encountered in the music literature being studied regardless of the class being taught. This is desirable especially if curiosity and interest is evinced by the student and the explanation aids in the musical experience at hand. This is what is meant by the *informal* teaching of music theory. It is granted that such informal presentation may not have a logical sequence of difficulty, nor assure the presentation of all of the important phases but is desirable even though done incidentally.

Formal music theory classes at the secondary level should be on an elective basis for the furtherance of musicianship. This class usually places emphasis upon the hearing and writing of various scales, intervals, chords and their progressions, and transposition, as well as the application of these items in singing and playing. Due to severe criticism of the content and techniques of instruction used in most existing theory classes, it is suggested that a detailed analysis be made of present practices to insure the accomplishment of musical goals.

Composition and Arranging. Composition means the production of original music and arranging means the adaptation or expansion of the music of others into a different or altered musical medium.

This course is to be found only in large metropolitan and vocational high schools. The membership will be small but those students who have talent in this area should have instruction available.

Schools granting credit for applied music often have a composition and arranging class as a required course to enhance the musical understanding and experience of these students who are preparing to be performers*

Assembly Singing. Singing usually has some place in all assembly programs and is of two distinct types, (a) that which is done for purposes of unification and recreation, and (b) that which has music instruction as its ultimate goal.

I. *Recreational Assembly Singing.* The camp-fire type of songs are usually used with emphasis on unison gusto. This may serve the purpose of quieting the students at the beginning of an assembly period but the musical value is negligible beyond the pleasure of emotional release through singing.

II. *Music Instruction.* There are certain aspects of music instruction which can be carried on effectively with an entire student body. This may take the form of a demonstration, the showing of a film, the listening to a selected radio or television program, special

*A splendid reference is the discussion by Noble Cain found in the *Music Education Source Book*, Music Educators National Conference. Chicago, Ill. 1947, Page 119–24.

concerts, lectures, or the singing of appropriate music literature. Even though the students may not be fully aware of the educational implications and the unusual musical contacts, the administration and music teacher in charge should see to it that these aspects are present.

For the sake of clarification, the content of the general assembly program which deals exclusively with music falls into three distinct types but these types may be combined effectively at times. They are, (a) where the entire student body participates as a unit, (b) where selected students or groups of students perform for the remainder of the student body, and (c) where outside musicians are presented.

Drum and Bugle Corps. This organization is popular with both student body and community and makes a special appeal to junior high school boys. This may be partially due to the wearing of smart uniforms and brisk formations.

Apart from the spectacular aspects, the drum and bugle corps may have some real musical possibilities because the transition from bugle to cornet or trumpet is easily made and drummers with ability to read score will be an asset to any school band or orchestra.

Baton Twirling. This is an adjunct used by some band directors and is an outgrowth of the popularity and attention given to the drum major of a marching band. Baton twirling is only an incidental to the many duties of a real drum major. The advisability of using several girl baton twirlers to accompany band maneuvers is questioned by some administrators as well as some band directors. The criticism seems to be directed at the time consumed by this activity which cannot be justified in the light of musical development.

Music Clubs

Some secondary schools have launched programs which require every student to affiliate with a club of his choice in an effort to assure a degree of informal social development. Activity or club periods are provided for during the regular school day if membership is a student requirement.

A music club may have some requirements for membership such as playing an instrument or singing a particular part but ideally membership should be open to any student interested in music. There may be two types of student membership such as performing and non-performing, as well as honorary members and faculty advisers.

138

The following list is suggestive of possible music club groupings.

1. Opera, or other Music Study Clubs
2. Record Collectors and Players Clubs
3. Accordion Club
4. Recital Club
5. MacDowell Club, or other specific composers
6. Piano Players Club
7. Club for Music Criticism
8. Radio and Television Fan Club
9. Guitar, Harmonica, Ukelele, Occarina Clubs
10. Folk Music and Dance Club.

School music clubs often serve as sponsors for musical activities for both school and community and may develop into real service organizations. It should be remembered that these clubs are *student* organizations and the more the students carry on all aspects of the club the more valuable it will be to the members.

SECTION III

RELATED AREAS

The four Chapters which comprise this Section are "Public Performance", "Scientific Devices", "Conducting", and "Rural School Music".

These areas have been isolated arbitrarily in order to give them additional emphasis. Their close relationship to the entire field of music education is vitally important because they involve activities, information, techniques, and skills, and because they contribute to the completeness of a well balanced program of music education.

20 PUBLIC PERFORMANCE*

No other department in public education is called upon to contribute at public affairs as often as the music department. This may be because music is recognized as an integrating element and is desired as a prelude to 'prepare the mind for the spoken word', or that the performance will be an enjoyable listening experience. There are many types of musical activities which are initiated by the school, often for the sole purpose of affording opportunity for students to appear before an audience. It is important that all public appearances should be analyzed from the viewpoint of the educational, musical, and social values to the student involved.

Why Give Public Performances? The chief reasons for public performances by school music groups which are sponsored and directed by the schools and music teachers may be stated briefly as follows.

(1) Cooperative planning and a united effort in reaching toward perfection for public presentation results in a marked rise in the performance ability of the pupils.

(2) Public performance usually calls for desirable collaboration of many departments of the school.

(3) In some schools a public performance is necessary to sell the music department to the student body.

(4) In a public performance, the parents and friends of the students take pleasure and pride in the work of the school, and disinterested persons may be 'sold' on the school music program.

(5) Musical performance not only raises the standard of appreciation in the performers, but if the performance is of high quality, it raises the standard of appreciation in the audience.

(6) Public performance where many individuals participate broadens the social outlook of the pupils.

(7) Some smaller communities must depend upon school music groups as the only live performances available to them.

What is an Audience? To give audience means simply to hear, to listen. It would follow that an audience may be composed of one

*Portions of this chapter are taken from the MUSIC EDUCATION SOURCE BOOK Chapter XXV, "Techniques and Ethics of Public Performances of School Music" which was written by one of the authors.

141

or many. And further, that the situation may be accidental or organized with the listeners absent or present. An alert music teacher will capitalize all types of audience situations for maximum values.

(1) No performing musician needs to be reminded that an audience of one may be a most challenging situation if the opinion and reaction of that one person is highly important to the performer. A vast audience may increase tension in the performer or it may be so large as to give only an impression of space instead of persons.

(2) The organized, planned, or scheduled performance presupposes adequate rehearsal time for carefully selected material, and that the stage setting is adequate and advantageous. This is usually regarded as a *public appearance*. However, if a friend, a parent, or school official visits a music class unannounced, an audience situation is created immediately.

(3) Due to radio and television, the unseen audience should be considered. Some performers seem to feel a lack of stimulation without the physical presence of listeners, others react favorably to the possibility of countless auditors.

(4) By the use of recording devices, it is possible for the performer to become the audience for his own performance. This audio technique has proved very valuable in teaching because the student quickly learns to accept the fact that 'this is what I did and this is how I sounded'.

Six Viewpoints

There are many legitimate reasons advanced both *for* and *against* public presentations by school music groups. These expressions come from six sources and vary according to the viewpoint of the group.

I. *The Administrator.* While interested in musical progress and educational goals, the administrator is vitally concerned with interrupted schedules, late rehearsals, community reactions, faculty friction, and anything else which affects the smooth running of the entire school.

A recent survey* reveals that school administrators agree that *careful* and *intelligent planning* can minimize all of his adverse criticisms. They further agree that in most cases, the acceptability of the public performances presented is used as a basis for their estimation of the music teacher in charge.

*A summary of this study which was made by one of the authors appears in the EDUCATIONAL MUSIC MAGAINE. Sept.–Oct. Issue 1951, Page 18.

Music educators grant that where the administrator is understanding and appreciative of the real values involved, active cooperation is present and this makes the load of preparation much lighter. The support and approval of those in charge of the over-all school program should be sought and assured before undertaking any large production.

II. *The Music Educator.* If the one in charge of teaching music in schools has had adequate preparation for the work he is doing, the presentation of individuals, ensembles, and larger groups will be an integral part of his yearly plan. At one extreme is the person who puts on a 'show' so that he may be in the lime-light as a director, and at the other extreme is the person who is so modest or shy that he avoids an appearance whenever possible. Likewise there are those who prefer to spend all teaching time in preparation for appearances and others who, due to a lack of proper appreciation of the developmental values, dislike to give the extra time and effort required to stage a finished production.

Most teachers are anxious for an audience so that the general public may know first hand the type of education through music which is taking place in their classroom, music department, or entire school.

III. *The Student.* Many music classes are organized with some type of performance in mind and this is taken for granted by the student. With very few exceptions, and perhaps these should be investigated psychologically, students enjoy stage appearances, foot-lights, make up, costumes, shows, concerts, pageants, parades, etc.

At heart, students are perfectionists, they want to appear well and will work untiringly to achieve the goals set for them. They have an idealistic sense of fairness and will respond beyond expectation provided *careful* and *intelligent planning* has taken place and the student participates in this planning so that he is fully aware of what his part in the entire program is to be.

IV. *The Professional Musician.* No one is more aware than the professional musician of the developmental benefits derived from repeated performances where perfection is the chief goal. Experience has convinced them that this is one of the best ways to control fear of audience and to establish self-confidence in the performer.

A very fine Code of Ethics* has been written cooperatively and adopted by the music educators of our country through their national organization, the Music Educators National Conference and the Musicians Union. Adherence to this code will enhance the work of both school and professional musicians.

*See Appendix B., page 174.

V. *The Parent.* Parental pride in the display of the accomplishments of their children is legitimate and understandable. Criticism usually centers around the method of selection for special or 'stellar' parts, too concentrated or too late rehearsals which leads to pupil exhaustion, and negative effects on grades in other school subjects. These criticisms do not exist when *careful* and *intelligent planning* is done.

The Parent Teachers Association has a splendid music department and has demonstrated their willingness to cooperate and support all school music activities. A wise music teacher knows that parents are generous almost to a fault in supporting anything which involves the welfare and progress of their children.

VI. *The Community.* In small communities where there are few or no touring musical events, the school has an obligation to serve. In larger cities where artist courses and symphony concerts are readily available, the community needs are not so great or perhaps non-existant. However, the same student needs for performance experience exists in both urban and rural communities.

It should be remembered that if the general public is asked to pay an admission fee, they have a right to expect an adequate performance. In most instances, a public performance is the only contact the community has with the music being taught in their school. Therefore, one should not be surprised if the entire school system as well as the entire music department is judged by one isolated performance on a basis of attention given to details of organization, demonstrated courtesy and general deportment. As much as one wishes that this were not the case, it is wisdom to be aware of the fact.

General Procedures of Preparation

There are two general procedures which are used to prepare for public performances.

(1) Fine classroom work over a period of time with finished work the natural outcome.

(2) Special rehearsals in preparation for a definite goal, the goal being a specific selection or selections to be presented upon a definite date for an audience.

For school initiated performances, it would be ideal if all selections presented were the result of splendid classroom development. Demands from outside the school often make it imperative to have special rehearsals in order to meet requests in an acceptable manner. It would follow then that either or both procedures are justifiable, depending upon the circumstances but the emphasis should be placed upon classroom work. Often a combination of the two methods is

144

used with a few special rehearsals following substantial classroom preparation.

The effect of the method used in preparation is apparent in the way the material is presented and upon the students involved. The thoroughness of the teacher's training is recognizable, and even though the results of unwise special rehearsals may not be apparent to the casual observer, the teachers and students will feel ill effects.

Requests for School Groups to Perform. The majority of requests for appearances of school musicians will come from the following sources: civic organizations, neighborhood and community events, local parades, local radio stations, churches, parent-teacher organizations, clubs, and in larger cities, visiting educational conventions.

In accepting invitations to appear in public, the method of preparation which would be necessary to meet the request should be well considered in the light of whether or not the participants will receive some educational benefit and whether the group served will receive a favorable impression of the music department and the entire school system. Discrimination in accepting and tact in refusing invitations must be exercised by the teacher and administrator.

General Suggestions

Unfair as it may seem, it should be recognized that one failure or sub-standard performance receives more comment from observers and critics than many fine successful appearances. Each of the following suggestions are important because success or failure may hinge upon it.

Type of Performance. From the viewpoint of student development, it would be well to plan so that during his progress through school, he has all types of musical performance experiences. This would preclude the giving of *all* types *every* school term, but it is highly desirable to have a term whose major performance interest is a concert, or a competition, or a festival, or a pageant, or a music-dramatic production, etc. This type of planning over a period of years will yield a well-balanced music program with varied and beneficial results for all concerned.

Selecting the Material. Before the material to be used is selected the following items should be investigated.

(1) Age and ability of participants.

(2) Time available and necessary for adequate preparation.

(3) Inherent musical worth, appeal to performers and audience.

(4) Development values; educational, social and musical.

(5) The types of performances which have been given previously and what materials were used.

(6) The season of the year, general appropriateness.

(7) Limitations of the stage and equipment where the performance will take place.

(8) Budget and expenditures involved.

(9) Active cooperation of other faculty and administration.

Selecting Students for Solo or Principal Parts. Principal or lead parts, solo assignments, etc., are tremendously important to the student, and if wisely done, will reduce greatly the amount of work necessary for a finished performance. Some items carry more weight than others in the final selection but all facets should be investigated.

1. Age and grade level—everything else being equal, the older and more advanced student should have preference.

2. Musical ability—the singing voice chosen must have the quality and range required; first chair student and soloist must have adequate technical skill.

3. Previous experience.

4. General physical condition of student.

5. Scholarship.

6. Personal traits; willingness, dependability, cooperation.

In many instances it is considered wise to use a committee of three when having try-outs for special assignments, but the thinking of the one who is to be directly in charge of rehearsals and performance should carry considerable weight.

Special Rehearsals. Every rehearsal should be planned with a specific accomplishment in mind and only those involved should attend. The rehearsals should be scheduled well in advance with the starting time and stopping time posted and carefully observed. It is advantageous to use the stage or platform where the production is to be given for as many rehearsals as possible.

The use of captains or leaders for designated responsibilities is a saving of time and helps to assure proper tempo of the whole performance. For example: the captain of the chorus would be in charge of mass entrances and exits for an operetta, a dance captain could learn the steps to be used and rehearse the dance line, section principals of the orchestra responsible for correct tuning, etc.

No rehearsal, special or otherwise, should keep children out after dark unless provision is made for safety in reaching their home. Rehearsals involving school children which last late into the night are inexcusable and should not be tolerated.

The final or dress rehearsal is maximum in importance and should proceed without interruptions. Notes should be taken during the performance and discussed after the students are off stage and seated. Only very necessary changes should be attempted at this time and they should be kept at a minimum. This final rehearsal should serve two purposes, (a) establish confidence beyond all doubt that the material is well in hand, and (b) that each individual knows and does exactly what is expected of him. Many a shaky performance is saved by the use of proper psychology at a final rehearsal.

Make-Up. A strong society or dry make-up is all that is necessary for non-dramatic appearances unless colored lighting is involved. The application of theatrical make-up is an art and requires a practiced technique if incongruity is to be avoided and the dramatic production enhanced.

Costuming. Choir robes and band uniforms are regarded by many as essentials. While it is granted that they contribute to eye appeal and aid the wearers in a feeling of belongingness, many groups meet these needs in a very inexpensive and effective way. For example: a girl's glee club in pastel shades, a mixed choir in white blouses and shirts, etc.

In dramatic productions, the costume should be of proper color, fit the figure of the one wearing it, be historically correct, aid the actor in feeling the character he is portraying, and add to the stage picture.

The costume mistress, costume master, chairman of the costume committee, and participating students will all function to better advantage if a chart of needed costumes is made well in advance and checked as arrangements are completed.

COSTUME CHART—EXAMPLE OF LISTINGS

CHARACTER	ACT I	ACT II	ACT III
Leading Lady	Shoes ( ) Dress ( ) Hat ( )	Same as Act I	Evening Dress ( ) Purse ( ) Long Gloves ( )
Leading Man	Dark Coat ( ) White Flannel Trowsers ( ) Bow Tie ( )	Business Suit ( ) Top Coat ( ) Gloves ( )	Tuxedo ( ) Dress Shirt ( ) Tie ( ) Shoes ( )
Dancing Chorus 1. Mary 2. Jane 3. Sally, etc.	Peasant Skirt ( ) White Blouse ( )		Pastel Colored Formal ( )

Staging: Lighting and Scenery. Elevations should be used whenever possible so that all may be seen by the audience and enable the participants to see the director. Improvised elevations must be checked for a wide margin of safety for the weight to be held.

Scenery and lighting combine to give an atmospheric background. They should establish locale, time of day, mood, and general aesthetic effect. Simplicity is always in good taste.

It should be remembered that the color of gelatin used in spot, flood, or any stage lighting equipment, affects the color of scenery and costumes. The following table of average color fusion may be helpful.*

Color of Pigment	Color of Light			
	Blue	Green	Amber	Red
Violet	Bluish violet	Dark blue	Dark orange	Reddish purple
Blue	Intense blue	Blue-green	Dark yellow-green	Bluish violet
Blue-green	Dark greenish blue	Green	Yellow-green tint	Blue-black
Green	Dark blue-green	Intense green	Intense yellow-green	Dark red
Yellow	Dark yellow-green	Yellow-green	Intense yellow	Orange
Orange	Very dark orange	Greenish yellow	Intense orange	Scarlet
Red	Dark reddish purple	Dark orange	Intense orange-red	Intense red
Purple	Purplish violet	Dark purple	Dark crimson	Purplish red

A cue sheet for the electrician should be prepared and rehearsed. It is important that complete lighting changes or adjustments should be an integral part of the dress rehearsal. It is much better to set the lights before the performance and use no adjustments or special effects than to have these changes take place at unscheduled moments.

Non-Musical Details. There are many details which have nothing to do with the actual music performance but which are very important to a successful production. Unless these are taken care of well in advance of the scheduled date of production, the success can easily be marred. The following should be considered as only a partial list. Further items will depend upon the local situation.

1. Publicity and printing of programs
2. Tuning of pianos
3. Having all instruments polished and put in best playing condition
4. Housing and supervision of groups while not on stage
5. Instructions to ushers as to proper time to seat late comers, etc.
6. Setting the right atmosphere for the performance such as no concessions sold in the building, etc.
7. Notification of police so that traffic will be under control, protection for box office, etc.
8. Car parking attendants
9. Putting ticket sale in hands of committee of teachers or student council
10. Inviting persons in the community who are particularly interested in music, special guests, etc.
11. Safe keeping of receipts after performance.

*Patterned after "Stage Lighting," by Theodore Fuchs. Little, Brown & Co., 1929, Page 130.

Types of Elementary School Programs

The following types of programs are suggested as suitable and desirable for production by elementary school children. Programs involving small children should be held in the afternoon or if an evening performance is demanded, it may well begin at an early hour.

1. Original pageants given in the school auditorium for schoolmates and parents. This may be an outlet for creative activities.
2. Pageant of American History Through Song.
3. Program built around the songs which have been memorized during a semester.
4. Pageant of United Nations using folk music, dances, and national anthems.
5. Festivities for special days such as Thanksgiving, Christmas, Washington's Birthday, Mother's Day, etc.
6. Operettas and cantatas.
7. Concerts by organizations such as the elementary choir, orchestra, and various small ensembles.

Block Form of Program. Any elementary program which lends itself to division into blocks of approximately eight to ten minutes in length, each one of which can be prepared by one elementary grade classroom, and then integrated by a commentary or continuity script, is ideal for small children. It may be enhanced with opening and closing numbers by a stationary chorus and orchestra. This type of performance allows for the maximum number of participants and requires a minimum of mass rehearsal.

Types of Secondary School Programs

The following suggestions deal with types of musical programs which are generally considered acceptable and desirable for production by secondary schools.

(1) Concerts demonstrating the work done in the classroom during a semester. These may be given during a school assembly period, as a vesper service, or an evening performance.

(2) Pageants in which many departments of the school collaborate. The following departments usually work together—Vocal and Instrumental Music, Speech, English, History, Dancing, Art, Clothing, and Manual Arts.

(3) Festivals in which all the schools of a city or a district cooperate. This may be the culmination of the year's work. If auditorium facilities permit, pupils of different age levels should participate in the same festival. Elementary choruses and instrumental groups are inspired by similar groups from junior and senior high school,

and in turn the teachers of secondary schools catch a glimpse of the musical experiences which precede high school experience when they hear groups from the elementary schools.

(4) Operas and operettas should be selected with discretion on a basis of musical worth. The majority of operettas can and should be produced in a minimum of four to six weeks. The educational advantages will justify the use of this much school time provided the work to be produced is carefully selected, efficiently rehearsed, and artistically presented. It is often desirable to use costume numbers and short musical skits in certain types of concert programs and thus incorporate some of the advantages of published shows.

(5) Cantatas and oratorios should be chosen with particular attention to the vocal difficulties they contain and the ability of the group which is to sing them. With careful handling, high school singers bring freshness and purity of tone to such masterpieces as Handel's *"Messiah"* and Haydn's *"Creation"*. This type of material charms the audience and raises the ideals of the singers to a remarkable degree.

A Critical Appraisal. From the negative point of view, an evaluation of public performances reveal that many fail to provide desirable educational, social, and musical experiences. An examination of the concert type of performance sometimes show that, (a) many are too long, (b) the material is cheap or chosen exclusively for audience appeal, and (c) the glorification of the conductor is frequently an apparent objective. Of the dramatic type of performance it may be said that, (a) the music is too difficult or too trivial, (b) the story content is often without meaning to the children participating, (c) the musical quality of the performance is inferior both instrumentally and vocally, (d) the exploitation of soloists is frequently harmful, and (e) the time consumed in rehearsing and the prolonged interference with the regular school schedule are disrupting forces in the school community.

While the above criticisms are deserved at times, many public performances succeed in providing valuable experiences and learning situations. Music literature of the highest type, both composed and folk, is found on the concert programs of many choral and instrumental groups. In many instances an appeal to the eye has not been neglected through the use of beautiful choir robes, appropriate stage settings, and impressive lighting effects. Notwithstanding the criticisms stated above, there are some good operettas in which the music and text both have intrinsic worth.

By grouping a variety of music programs within the same week, music festivals of astonishing proportions are often developed. This festival may be done in cooperation with National Music Week and serve a fine community purpose.

150

Summary

Because public performances involve so many students, other faculty and the entire community, the reactions are easily observed. Practically all adverse comments are the result of inadequate planning or poor judgment and are directed chiefly at the method or material rather than the activity.

Regular instrumental and vocal concerts should continue to be an integral part of the educational program of music education. The benefits to be capitalized are standards maintained by selection based upon aptitude and interests, educational guidance and educational materials. Dangers to be avoided are unwise use of show pieces, exploitation of especially talented students, limited variety of music, too lengthy program, and extreme ambition in symphonic or choral music.

More use should be made of large performing groups which will stimulate cooperation not only of the instrumental and vocal music departments but of the entire teaching staff and student body. Contemporary American music should be included whenever feasible.

Published productions and entertainments such as operettas, cantatas, etc., should be selected with discretion and used for educational ends. Some of the assets derived from the use of special lighting, costuming and scenery may be utilized to enhance certain types of concert programs.

Music educators are urged to plan at least one annual program in which all departments of the school cooperate on a large scale. Such programs are natural concomitants of the socialized program of present-day schools. The ideas, materials, preparation, and final presentation should stem from the regular school work.

The real measure of worth of any and all public performances should be in terms of the educational, social, and musical development of those participating.

21 SCIENTIFIC DEVICES

There are two major groups of scientific devices which have proven very valuable in the field of music education. The *first* group consists of numerous tests and measures which deal with native musical talent, music adjustment, and musical accomplishment. The *second* group consists of machines or mechanical devices, some of which are designed for testing purposes and others whose chief purposes are to assist or enhance audio-visual presentation.

Tests and Measures

Music entered the field of testing among the very earliest of all school subjects, but has been one of the slowest subjects in the curriculum to profit by the findings of tests and and measures. Many explanations have been given for this delay but the one generally advanced is the thought that music, as an art, deals with a type of talent which has been held beyond the confines of that which may be classified and measured. Upon close investigation, the real reason in some instances seems to be that those teaching music are blissfully satisfied with what they are accomplishing and also the way in which they are accomplishing it. Realizing the breadth and scope of scientific investigation, they have been afraid and so continue complacently in a musical rut. Alert and scientifically minded music educators have attempted to isolate those parts of music which are measurable and to make deductions from the data yielded by tests and measures.

To date, the subject of music has gone through the same stages of development in the testing activities as have spelling, arithmetic, reading, and other subjects in the curriculum. Scientific investigations in music have found results which are analogous to some of the findings in these other branches. One outstanding similarity is that many unimportant items can be eliminated entirely from the curriculum with profit, and that other items need not occupy the place of importance which they traditionally have held. These eliminations would give time for things which have been found to be more essential. The grade placement of many fundamental music activities has been challenged.

Prognostic or innate capacity tests were the first type of music test developed and these were followed by achievement tests in comparatively large numbers. The knowledge side, or the achievement side of music can be and is measured with as much skill and accuracy as any other subject because the mechanical and ordinary achievement phases of music instruction lend themselves very readily to testing.

The sociological and psychological area involving musical adjustment or sufficiency is the most recent to be investigated. These research workers recognize that there are intangible elements present in music but they are not permitting this fact to deter them from trying to isolate factors which are measurable or to deal with combinations of factors which have recognizable effects.

There has been a wide overlapping into the field of music from other interested groups. The physicists have made many tests in the realm of sound and acoustics; those interested in health and medicine have investigated lung capacity, posture, hearing, sight, muscular control, and phases of mental health. The therapeutic effects of music on mood and the treatment of psycho-neurotic cases as well as those in penal institutions are receiving appropriate attention with many very definite and satisfactory findings. Physical education has concerned itself chiefly with the many aspects of rhythm, while those interested primarily in English have made contributions to the field of music by their investigations in thought and word content of songs as well as enunciation and pronunciation. Music educators should strive to utilize these findings.

Native Music Talent Tests

The talent potentialities with which one is endowed at birth are recognized as one of the elements which have much to do with the extent of musical accomplishment which the individual attains. There are two well-known tests of musical sensitivity or innate musical talent. They are, (a) The Seashore Measures of Musical Talent, and (b) The Kwalwasser-Dykema Test. There has been considerable evaluation and comparison of these two tests. A fairly new contribution to this area is Dr. E. Thayer Gaston's Test of Musicality.

Seashore Measures of Musical Talent. This test was constructed by Dr. Carl E. Seashore and has been called an 'epoch making' work in the history of music education. It was first presented in 1920 and was revised in 1939. It is based upon two premises, namely, (a) that every person has some degree of musical talent probably distributed in the population in conformity to the normal curve, and (b) that musical talent is not a single capacity but is made up of numerous specific capacities, many of which are independent of one another.

The revised Seashore Test has two series, Series A to be used with unselected groups, and Series B, designed for testing of musicians and prospective or actual students of music. The test is administered by use of recordings and contains six divisions. They are (1) Pitch, (2) Loudness, (3) Time, (4) Timbre, (5) Rhythm, and (6) Tonal Memory. The test is easy to administer and to score. Established norms are available.

Kwalwasser-Dykema Test. This test was constructed by Dr. Peter W. Dykema and Dr. Jacob Kwalwasser and is commonly referred to as the "K-D" Test. Like the Seashore Test, the K-D Test is administered by the use of recordings. It is composed of the following parts: (1) Tonal Memory, (2) Quality Discrimination, (3) Intensity Discrimination, (4) Tonal Movement, (5) Time Discrimination, (6) Rhythmic Discrimination, (7) Pitch Discrimination, (8) Melodic Taste, (9) Pitch Imagery, and (10) Rhythm Imagery. This test has printed score sheets and is quite easy to administer and score. Established norms are available.

Gaston Test of Musicality. (Third Edition.) Constructed and revised by Dr. E. Thayer Gaston, this test purports to indicate the musical personality of the individual tested. It is an attempt to search out for interpretation both directly and indirectly, the drawing power of music for the child or student, to determine his awareness of musical structure and to establish the extent of his response to musical situations.

The test consists of a four page test form, a manual of directions and a scoring key which are used in connection with an album of recordings. Standardized norms have been prepared.

Music Achievement Tests

Most tests in this area deal with factual material and are readily adaptable to the 'paper and pencil' technique. There are more than fifty available tests which claim to measure music achievement or accomplishment. They vary from tests which have been statistically treated for reliability, validity, objectivity, and the power to differentiate, to a compilation composed of questions to which some individual thinks students should know the answers.

An achievement test may be written by a local music teacher to ascertain the extent to which the students he has instructed has retained the information. There is always a place for a test which is locally designed for local use but it should not be confused with

154

a standardized test. Standardized tests have survived statistical analysis of various forms and usually have established norms which can be used for comparing local scores with a wider or national level of accomplishment. Unless a printed test has a safe reliability and validity, it should not be used because it has little basis for meaningfulness or comparison.

In selecting a music achievement test for use, all possibilities for variation in administration should be considered. For example, if notes are to be played or sung by the one giving the test, there is no guarantee that the tempo will be what the author desired or even that the correct time values will be given to the notes used. Some tests have been weakened by requiring the testee to do two or more things at the same time. For example, the student may be asked to decide whether two selections are identical and if not, whether it was the rhythm, melody, or harmony that was altered.

Achievement tests can serve two purposes, (1) to verify the knowledge of students taking the test, and (2) the effectiveness of the teaching being done. Both purposes have educational meaning and are important to music education.

Many music achievement tests are suitable for 'pre-teaching' and 'post-teaching' use. They may be given at the beginning of a term and re-given at the end of the term. The difference in individual scores would give an indication of the progress made during the term.

All music teachers should continue to write tests for their local situation but it is desirable at times to use standardized tests in order to evaluate their own teaching in terms of student accomplishment on a wider basis. No one achievement test in music should be used to the exclusion of all others as there is safety and statistical significance in using several different tests with the same group.

Music Adjustment Inventory

The Music Adjustment Inventory was constructed by Dr. Hazel B. Nohavec and was released in 1943 after six years of investigation and refinement. It was constructed in an attempt to evaluate some of the outcomes of systematic music instruction and was designed to cover to some extent that area of music education which deals not with native musical talent nor acquired music knowledge or skills, but with the general adjustment or sufficiency of the individual in average or normal life relationships and situations that involve music. It has been called an instrument to measure the sufficiency of musical training for musical needs.*

*See foot-note, page 90.

An intensive investigation and survey of all the available printed tests which could serve music education lead to the following conclusions.

(1) That music educators need to equip themselves so as to be able to administer music tests, aid in devising and revising test materials, and most important of all, to be able to interpret and apply the findings.

(2) That native music ability tests while not without flaws, are sufficiently refined to warrant universal use.

(3) That a separate or single score should never be used as a definite and final talent classification.

(4) That the scores on any music achievement test should be interpreted in the light of the way the test was constructed.

(5) That there is need for improvement in the construction of music tests both as to type and content.

(6) That the more skillful the technique is in the use of music tests, the better the yielded results.

(7) That it is highly desirable to use a battery of several tests in the various areas of music before any diagnosis or recommendation is made.

SOME AUDIO-VISUAL DEVICES

The alert teacher always has appealed to the ear and the eye to enhance and strengthen his teaching but the advent of numerous mechanical devices has given a new impetus to the use of audio-visual materials and techniques of presentation. The influence of mechanical devices as teaching aids is far-reaching and has not been utilized to its fullest extent in the field of music education.

Phonograph and Recordings. A good reproducing machine is necessary equipment for the effective teaching of many phases of music in all grades. Commercially made recordings are indispensable in presenting listening lessons and rhythmic activities. They serve ideally as patterns of performance. Transcriptions are finding their way rapidly into school use. As the use of the phonograph and recordings has been stressed previously in connection with various grade levels and activities, it is sufficient here to list them as mechanical devices.

Motion Pictures. Most schools are now equipped to show educational motion pictures. These machines may be of two kinds, a projector capable of showing the standard commercial films or a small portable projector using a 16mm film. The catalog of desirable educational films is increasing rapidly.

Music educators should keep themselves informed about the music used in commercial films which are shown in regular movie theatres. It is their duty to recommend those films worthy of musical consideration. The chief criticism of commercial films on music subjects is that in some instances there has been a lack of complete authenticity in the material presented.

Closely related to the motion picture are film strips and slides. These are best suited to classroom use. There are eight major types of film and projector equipment each one of which serves a specific purpose.

(1) Standard Slide Projector—for standard sized glass slides.

(2) Miniature Slide Projector—for glass slides two inches square.

(3) Film Strip Projector—for showing pictures in sequence on film strips of twelve to forty-eight inches in length.

(4) Opaque Projector—reflects light by a series of mirrors; pictures, material or other objects may be used.

(5) Micro-film Projector—gives an eighteen inch square reflected projection of a book page or other printed material.

(6) Silent Movie Projector—reflects pictures from film in rapid succession.

(7) Sound Movie Projector—similar to (6) but with sound track.

(8) Combination Projector—many machines combine several of the above features.

Radio and Television. The reception of music by radio and television is a very important part of music education. The chief obligation of the school may be briefly stated as: (1) the schools must teach children so that they can choose intelligently radio and television programs of music which are worthy of their listening time, and (2) the schools should make use of the educational programs available during school time which is commensurate with the time required and the desirability of the material presented.

Further availability of "F-M", frequency modulation broadcasting, has many implications for the immediate future as it is to be used largely for educational purposes. Television will increasingly play a part in the over-all music education program as schools become equipped to use this medium.

Audio Frequency Oscillator. A machine used to test pitch accuracy. It can produce small differences in intensity and frequency.

Audiometer. An instrument used for the testing of hearing ability or acuity.

Metronoma. A tempo indicator controlled by electronics and is useful in identifying and correcting time deficiencies.

Mirrorphone. A recording device of about one minute and so constructed that an immediate play back is possible. The recorded material may be erased by the pressing of a button.

Oscillograph. An electrically controlled instrument to be used in remedial work in tone quality. Any deviation in timbre may be detected visually.

Spotit and Phonoscope. Simple instruments to be used on standard recordings and enables one to locate specific passages as desired.

Sound Level Meter and Sound Analyzer. This instrument measures the intensities of various frequencies and is, an aid in the analysis of frequencies found in complex sounds.

Strobescope. An instrument to check objectively the accuracy of intonation. It is usable for both voices and musical instruments. It is sometimes called the "Strobeconn" and is helpful in any situation which involves pitch or frequency.

Wire and Tape Recorders. Recorders with good fidelity capable of immediate play back and erasure are one of the most helpful of all devices.

Summary

The cost of certain mechanical devices makes it rather impractical for most schools to own them, but some very reliable machines are within the budget of the average school. A few companies will supply machines on a rental basis. Many state universities are quite well equipped with machines of all types and it is often possible for students in a neighboring area to use them.

Mechanical devices are impersonal and can be a tremendous aid in analysis and testing certain phases of music and musical ability, as well as a means for teaching music. It is the chief objective evaluation that a performer can make of his own work.

22 CONDUCTING

An ancient manuscript from the fourteenth century depicts a Minnesinger supposed to be Heinrich von Meissen, with a stick in his hand directing a group of musicians. It can be supposed that this was a recognized feature of group performance in these early times. During the seventeenth century and early eighteenth century, the conductor usually played the organ or harpsichord and made such nods and gestures as were possible to keep the performers 'on the beat'.

By the beginning of the nineteenth century, the art of conducting had progressed to include interpretation and the advent of Mendelssohn, Liszt, Wagner, and Berlioz, served to focus attention upon the techniques of conducting and the conductor as a person.

Effective present day conducting of music groups depends largely upon the personality of the conductor, his adequacy of skill in conducting techniques, and his general musicianship.

The Conductor as a Person. The personal qualities and qualifications for a successful conductor may be briefly stated as follows.

(1) Muscianship
(2) Wide experience with music literature and its performance
(3) An agreeable personality to include tact, a sense of humor, and a poise which is conducive to leadership
(4) Alertness, presence of mind, and self control
(5) Imagination to conceive perfection
(6) Organization and planning ability to carry through to perfection.

Each one of the above six items is of great importance and a personal deficiency in any one area could make the difference between success and failure of the individual as a conductor.

Confidence and respect can be given to both performers and audience by the posture of the conductor, his manner of entrance and exit, and his acknowledgement of applause. These items should be practiced until they become automatic. Conducting has certain aspects of legitimate showmanship but must be based upon a knowledge of audience and group psychology, and should never become 'show-off-ship'. It should be remembered always that the music being performed is the really important thing and that a good conductor is never obtrusive personally.

Directing Young Children. The classroom singing of elementary school children requires direction to the extent that the beginning and ending is in unison, and that the tempo and dynamics are indicated when needed. This should be done with the arm and hand in an inconspicuous manner without the use of a baton. Facial expression, nods, and limited gestures usually will be sufficient. Children should be encouraged to sing expressively by giving them an opportunity for discussion of the mood, meaning, or story, which is to be portrayed by their singing of a particular song.

Leading Informal Music Groups. The leaders of informal music groups which are performing for recreational purposes are often called 'starters'. This well describes their duties, and regardless of the age of the participants, the techniques of directing are quite similar to those used for young children. Perhaps the arm is used more to indicate the rhythmic flow of the music. Enthusiasm, inspiration, personal charm, and a sense of humor are essential for successful informal leadership but musicianship is also an important requisite.

Directing Bands, Orchestras, Choruses, and Choirs. There are some music educators who still insist that a decided difference exists in basic conducting techniques used for the directing of vocal and instrumental music, likewise, some believe that there is a difference between techniques which are effective for rehearsal and those which are proper for public performances. While a small variation may be permissable, it must be recognized that there are basic concepts of conducting techniques which are common to all situations where music is prepared and presented with inspiration, accuracy, and finesse. The remainder of this chapter is concerned with these fundamental techniques and suggestions for general improvement of the music educator as a conductor.

Minimum Conducting Techniques

The general function of a conductor has three phases, namely, (a) the determination of the desired or proper interpretation of the musical selection to be presented, (b) the preparation of the performers for presentation of this pre-determined interpretation, and (c) the actual conducting of the performance.

The responsibility for indicating tempo, dynamics, phrasing, rhythmic structure, attacks and releases, and the over-all mood of the selection, belongs to the conductor. These will be conveyed largely by a rather conventional arm and hand movement. As the conductor responds to the music within himself, he will automatically change facial expression and vary his muscle tension, thus he will transfer to his group significant inspiration for interpretation. Sincerity and truth are important because superficiality is easily detected and brings forth an opposing reaction.

Basically, the right arm indicates the tempo and beat detail, and the left arm is used to indicate the interpretation. The length of the beat stroke is closely related to the type of interpretation being indicated. Each arm and hand may be used to enhance or emphasize the work of the other provided it does not become wild, meaningless, and continuous flapping of both arms. It is ludicrous and distracting to see arms used in apposition with the head bobbing downward as the arms are outstretched. It is granted that some recognized professional conductors use motions which would be confusing and unsuitable for use with amateur performers. One should strive for meaningful motions and a happy medium between stiff or angular motions and too relaxed or stirring motions. No audible sound such as snapping the fingers, humming, counting, patting the foot, or tapping the rack is good form.

Basic Outline of Beats. The first requisite for any beat outline is that it be clear and meaningful. While basic beat outlines are uniform there are some accepted variations to details of the beat pattern and it is important that each individual conductor adopt a 'routine of details' and use it systematically at all times, rehearsal and performance, alike.

The regular indication of time units as indicated by the meter signature at the beginning of a selection may be classified as: (a) duple: measure units in two's, (b) triple: measure unit in three's, and (c) quadruple: measure unit in four's. Each of these may be extended where one beat motion includes three secondary units. For example: the basic movement for $\frac{6}{8}$ meter may be the same as for $\frac{2}{4}$ meter providing the rhythmic flow of the music is duple, or in two's.

In the following diagrams of basic angular beat outlines it should be noted that the *one,* or primary accent beat is a down-beat regardless of classification, that the *second* beat is *away* from the body in triple measures but *across* the body in quadruple measures. The final beat of the measure unit will be upward and should return the arm in position for the down-beat which is to follow immediately. Fluidity will soften the angles of the outline but the fundamental direction of the beat must be maintained.

(1) Duple—Count 1 is downward,
count 2 is upward. $(\frac{2}{2}, \frac{2}{4}, \frac{2}{8})$

(2) Triple—Count 1 is downward,
count 2 is away from the body,
count 3 is upward. $(\frac{3}{2}, \frac{3}{4}, \frac{3}{8})$

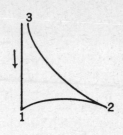

(3) Quadruple—Count 1 is downward,
count 2 is across the body,
count 3 is back across the body
and extends away from the body,
count 4 is upward. $(\frac{4}{2}, \frac{4}{4}, \frac{4}{8})$

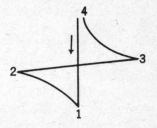

(4) Extended Duple—basic outline same as for duple measure. If tempo demands 4 beats instead of 2, the quadruple outline is used. If the beat unit in $\frac{6}{8}$ meter is a dotted quarter note (♩.), the basic outline is that of the duple, but if each count of the measure needs to be indicated the outline should be

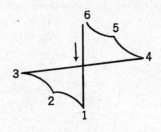

(5) Extended Triple—basic outline same as for triple measure, $(\frac{9}{4}, \frac{9}{8}, \frac{9}{16})$, unless each count of the measure needs to be indicated, then the outline should be

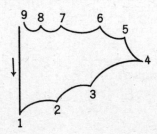

(6) Extended Quadruple—basic outline same as for quadruple measure, ($\frac{12}{4}$, $\frac{12}{8}$, $\frac{12}{16}$), unless each count of the measure needs to be indicated, then the outline should be

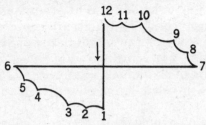

The Preparatory Beat—Attack and Release. The preparatory attack beat is considered the all important beat because it indicates the exact instant when the attack is to be made. It is used for initial attacks as well as for subsequent attacks such as after a rest, an interlude, etc. Some directors of inexperienced groups begin with the down-beat of the measure preceding the one in which the attack occurs and train the group to watch for a signal by his left hand for exact time of attack. This may be permissable in rehearsal when the selection is first introduced but can result in awkward pauses or faulty timing if continued. The use of one preparatory beat made in the direction the preceding beat would take is considered desirable for both amateur and professional performers.

Release of tone is equal in importance with attack of tone and may be indicated effectively with a slight but precise wrist movement. It must be exact and should be preceded by a preparatory warning. In some instances by the time a selection is ready for performance, a slight nod or change of facial expression may suffice for the preparatory release.

Shall a Baton Be Used? A baton held in the hand is actually an extension of the arm which allows the beat to be seen more clearly. It would follow, then, that in situations which involve a large number of performers such as a festival chorus accompanied by an orchestra, the use of a baton would be advantageous and perhaps imperative. Further, its use may give confidence to both performers and conductor. There are situations where a baton in the hand may prove to be detrimental; for example, certain types of phrase indication and nuances especially with vocal groups. The decision to use or not to use a baton while conducting should be on the basis of whether its use or disuse will result in a satisfactory musical performance and not on the basis of presence or lack of proficiency in baton technique.

Shall a Podium Be Used? The purpose which a podium serves is to elevate the conductor so that all performers may see his directing. The presence or absence of risers, the size of the performing group, and the height of the conductor will be determining factors. It is equally out of place to use a podium when not needed as it is not to use one when really necessary.

Techniques for Interpretation. While emphasis has been given to various conducting techniques which are centered in the right arm and hand, the importance of the left hand should not be minimized. The two will be combined or coordinated at times for climactic points, however, cues, details of dynamics, changes in tempo, and finesse of balance, should be controled by movements made by the left arm and hand.

The interpretation of a musical selection is concerned largely with the following.*

(1) *"Style.* The general style and character of the composition will largely determine its interpretation. Haydn's music demands different presentation from Debussy's music. The well-prepared conductor is acquainted with music history and tradition, and considers the various factors which determine the style of a given composition and therefore the general nature of its presentation.

(2) *Tempo.* Probably no single element so effects the successful presentation of a composition as the selection of the correct tempo. Tempo is far more than merely determining the general rate of speed to be taken; it means a flexible sense of all the finer modifications of speed which bring out the inner significance of the musical movement. The nature of the music, as dance form, historic period, descriptive effect, lyric flow, and many other elements enter into the determination of effective tempo. The words in vocal music, musical figuration, character of the melody and harmony, and numerous other factors help to decide the tempo as much as do tempo markings, metronome indications, and descriptive terms employed by the composer or editor.

(3) *Mood.* The mood of a musical work determines the performance with respect to (a) dynamics and accentuation, (b) tone color, and (c) legato versus staccato effects. The conductor must discover the composer's meanings and employ such variations in these elements of performance as shall best carry out the message of the music. In well written vocal music, the words should give a key to the details of the proper mood.

(4) *Form.* The musical structure is a large factor in determining the interpretation. Correct and effective phrasing involves consciousness of phrase relationship and the 'rise and fall' within a phrase. Contrasting sections should receive contrasting treatment. Climaxes are dependent upon structural proportions, both for climaxes within each section and the grand climax of the entire work.

---

*Osborne McConathy, Russell V. Morgan and George L. Lindsay. *Music the Universal Language.* Silver Burdett Company, New York, 1941. Page 293.

(5) *Articulation.* By 'articulation' is meant not only diction in vocal music but bowings and tongueings in instrumental music. The conductor must see to it that the most careful attention is given to clean, artistic articulation, not only as a necessary element in distinct performance, but as an essential means for presenting the desired ideas and moods of the composition.

(6) *Imagination and Feeling.* Above all, interpretation demands imagination and feeling for the conductor must be able to project himself into the picture, to participate in the situation or mood of the music, and to identify himself with the composer's inner intentions.''

Student Conductors. Every student group has one or more members who have qualifications for musical leadership. It is well to designate, or assign by try-out, a student conductor for most school music organizations and if the membership warrants it, an assistant student conductor.

The chief duties of such a student conductor would be to assist the instructor with any responsibilities delegated to him and to be in charge of the group in the absence of the instructor. As the reliability and conducting ability of this student develops, he should be allowed to conduct at school assemblies, pep rallies, etc. Proper credit in programming should be given to those students who serve in this capacity.

Summary

(1) While there may be some elements of native talent in conducting, it should be regarded as a skill which needs to be studied and practiced.

(2) There are regulations regarding basic conducting movements which should not be violated.

(3) Students of all ages can be taught to respond to a conductor provided they understand what is indicated by every conductive movement.

(4) The character of the beat as well as the direction of the beat is important in the indications for interpretation.

(5) The music needs to be analyzed carefully by the conductor for style, tempo, mood, and form, *before* it is presented to a group for rehearsal.

(6) Performance of musical selections may be a thrilling experience for an audience, singers, players, and conductor, provided the conductor knows what he should do and does it in a proper fashion.

23 RURAL SCHOOL MUSIC

More than one-half of the school children in the United States attend rural schools. In many respects the musical needs of this large group of children are not being met adequately at the present time. Music education, as a part of general education is the prerogative of every rural child and the inequality of musical opportunity caused by residential location should be and is being overcome rapidly. The universal music education of this very large group of boys and girls is beginning to receive proper attention by music educators. When this problem of equal musical opportunity is solved, the slogan, "Music for Every Child" will become a reality.

Many states have passed laws which require that music, art, and hygiene be taught in every rural school and other states are rapidly following this lead. Approximately one-third of our states employ state supervisors of music at the present time and, in some states which do not have this service as yet, county supervisors of music are employed. A few states enjoy the services of both state and county music supervisors.

The State Organization Plan. In order to have equal instruction and opportunity for instruction in music throughout a state, a state organization must be effected. This may be conducted along either of two plans, namely: (1) State Music Supervisor or Consultant with an assistant for each county in the state, or (2) State Music Supervisor or Consultant with assistants assigned according to population.

Either plan would tend to give uniform opportunity for music and material, but the latter plan would equalize the number of visits made to each school by the consultant or special music teacher. With state organization in effect, every rural school would be kept informed of the newest ideas, methods and materials. Equipment, such as reproducing machines, records, charts, pictures, and other audiovisual aids, could be circulated from a central point, thus minimizing the expense with a maximum of utility. Children attending the elementary grades in a rural school would find no adjustment difficulty when they attend a town or city high school, as all would have been instructed along similar lines and under the over-all supervision of one person. A centralization of the administrative work would result in a higher degree of efficiency.

The County Organization Plan. Where no state consultant of music is employed or where no state law has been enacted, the county plan of organization has proved usable and successful. This plan is similar to the state organization but each county functions independently. The schools are so few in some counties as to require the services of only one music supervisor or teacher while others would demand the services of several assistants to carry out an effective music program. The county plan of organization would not tend to equalize the music program of the state as a whole. The consolidation program for rural schools, as well as the extent of hard surfaced roads will be factors in any county supervision plan.

Four Prime Factors

The problem resolves itself into three major questions: namely, (1) how to promote music in areas where it is not now offered or where the offering is inadequate, (2) how to secure adequate music training for those who intend to teach in rural schools, and (3) how to improve the music teaching of those who are now rural school teachers.

As no two situations are identical, the factors which control the situation are worthy of investigation. There are four prime factors to be considered and the cooperation of these four can bring about an active rural school music program in a minimum of time. They are, (1) the state and county superintendents of public instruction, (2) the rural school teacher, (3) the school board or board of directors, and (4) the patrons and pupils.

I. *The State and County Superintendent of Public Instruction.* When the superintendent in charge of instruction is aware of the importance of music in the life of every child, cooperation is assured. The first step is to secure adequate finances and then the employment of a trained person to lead and direct the music in the schools. This will assure an organized program under authorized leadership.

The basic functions of the rural music supervisor or consultant, whether they be employed by the state or county, can be stated briefly in seven broad items.

(1) To prepare a workable program in music education which will include all types of music activities for all schools in the area supervised.

(2) To aid rural teachers in acquiring the skill to teach their music in an effective manner.

(3) To aid in securing necessary equipment and materials for each school.

167

(4) To assist in making the use of materials, such as text books, recordings, radio programs, etc., increasingly effective.

(5) To organize and promote large area concerts, contests and festivals.

(6) To secure cooperation of various groups in sponsoring musical organizations and activities.

(7) To serve as an agent in informing the community of the importance of music and its need in child development.

II. *The Teacher.* Ideally, the rural teacher should be able to play the piano in an acceptable fashion, have an agreeable singing voice, and have had sufficient training in methods of presenting music to a class composed of children of different age levels. It has been demonstrated that much can be done by average rural teachers if they firmly believe in the values of music as a technique and an art so that the children will become intelligent consumers of music.

Rural teachers can create an interest in music on the part of the students and also the community. They can carry out to the best of their ability, the program as outlined by the state or county music consultant and in the absence of any supervision, can take considerable initiative in making their music needs known.

III. *The School Board or Board of Directors.* The school board or board of directors must be in sympathy with what the rural teacher is trying to accomplish musically for the children in the district. It is their responsibility to furnish adequate equipment such as music books, records, phonograph, radio, etc., and to support actively the entire music program.

In selecting a new teacher, it is recommended that the musical ability and training of the applicant be investigated.

IV. *The Patrons and Pupils.* The patrons and pupils constitute the community. Rural parents are anxious that their children have all the educational privileges and opportunities that are offered to any child anywhere. The National Congress of Parents and Teachers has clubs in almost every school community. This is a valuable organization to the cause of music and its members always stand ready to assist.

Other adult organizations vitally interested in the rural child are the National Education Association through its Rural Education Service, the National Federation of Music Clubs, the Grange and the Farm Bureau. These all sponsor music activities and can give valuable aid.

Three organizations, the Future Farmers of America, Future Homemakers of America, and the 4-H Clubs have encouraged musical activities for rural youth and are recognized both state-wide and nationally.

Many colleges and universities offer courses in music for rural teachers and other institutions would be glad to offer such courses if requested to do so.

Types of Rural Schools

There are two major types of rural school organization which should be considered. They are, (1) the Consolidated School, and (2) the One Room School. The kind of music program used will depend upon the type of rural school.

The Consolidated School. A consolidated school may be composed of either elementary or secondary grades, or both. However, the majority are consolidated high schools where children who have completed the offerings of a local rural school are transported to a larger school plant which is supported by several individual rural school districts. These have united to form a consolidated school district.

Consolidation eliminates the problem of small numbers of students and multi-grade classrooms. Regular music teachers usually have charge of the music classes and the same plans, activities and methods of procedure can be used as have been found universally successful.

One Room School. A one room rural school may have children attending it in any or all grades from the first through the eighth. The number of children attending may vary from four or five to over thirty. All the teaching of all the subjects in all the grades is handled by one teacher.

The general practice for the extension of any movement has been for it to start in the cities and then radiate to the surrounding territory, using the same materials and methods. This must not be true of the music that is extended until it reaches the one-room structures. Plans must be formulated with the rural idea as the center. Instead of complaining of conditions, such as distance, lack of time etc., a plan should and can be formulated, not only to meet, but to capitalize upon the conditions as they actually exist. Many of the obstacles which are believed to be present, in reality do not exist but such limitations as finances, small number of students, several grades in one room, and inadequate training of the teacher must be recognized.

Automobiles and good roads have eliminated distance and isolation to a certain extent. Radio, television, and reproducing machines have helped in the way of providing fine musical material. Text book companies have provided music books for use in multi-graded rooms. As time is always found for the things that are deemed most important, the problem of a crowded daily schedule will solve itself in each individual case. Many plans have been tried but no one plan or formula can be recommended for all rural schools in all rural communities. The following suggestions should prove helpful to a teacher in an isolated community.

Suggestions for the Isolated Rural Teacher

Where no state or county organization exists, it is necessary for the isolated rural teacher, aided by the county superintendent of public instruction, to carry on the music work. The following suggestions can quite readily be carried out by the average teacher.

(1) See to it that the children know the words as well as music to many patriotic and folk songs.

(2) All children can be taught the characteristic differences between march rhythm, dance rhythm, and the rhythm of a lullaby.

(3) Attention can be called to whether the music is high or low, soft or loud, fast or slow.

(4) At times it is well not to point out every mistake, particularly at the time it is made, but let part of the attention be fixed upon the beauty of the melody or selection at hand.

(5) All children should be taught a few musical terms so that at least they can read a printed music program with intelligence and understanding. Care must be taken not to overwhelm them with a hopeless maze of technicalities.

(6) There is a rich field in the rural community for correlation of music with nature, for example, the imitation of bird calls, work songs, etc.

(7) If money is to be spent for recordings, consult the teacher in the neighboring district in order to buy selections that she does not have. An exchange can be made for a few weeks which will be helpful to all concerned.

(8) Perhaps two districts wish to stage an operetta. By using the same one, the expense of costumes and scenery can be cut in half.

(9) Community singing has a broad cultural value as well as a good psychological effect. Informal singing should be encouraged.

(10) A community orchestra or band, even though a small one, is a wonderful asset. Informal groups of players on social instruments such as the accordion, guitar, banjo, etc., can do much for entertainment and will lead to other instrumental music activities.

(11) If music teachers are available, children should be encouraged to take private lessons on any and all kinds of instruments. As soon as they are at all proficient, these children may perform at school.

170

(12) It is well to divide the pupils of a one-room rural school into two groupings according to ability, those doing rote work would constitute one group and those capable of reading notes would constitute the second group. This plan of organization will simplify many problems and is advised even at the sacrifice of the number of music lessons possible during a given week.

(13) With a little organization and cooperative planning, a program can be arranged whereby neighboring schools would prepare material for ten to twenty minutes. Then, at a given time and place, a combined program can be presented with no general rehearsal necessary. It is very helpful to see and hear other groups because it tends to raise performance standards.

(14) One ingenious teacher took a step toward keeping fresh material for her school by using songs on the even numbered pages of the music book for one term, and the songs on the odd numbered pages the following term.

(15) Most of the time in the rural school music period should be used in helping the children to sing well many appropriate songs, to listen intelligently and understandingly, and to form a preference for the best in music. As much sight reading should be taught as time will permit but care must be taken not to hamper the emotional side of music by long-drawn drills on signs and symbols.

(16) The phonograph and radio are indispensable to an effective rural school music program.

The Use of Radio and Television

All major radio and television networks carry educational programs designed for school use. Many state and local stations have programs devoted entirely to music, or programs in which music is an integral part, broadcast especially for school reception. Numerous state universities and colleges maintain broadcasting stations and have organized rural school programs.

The major broadcasting companies publish a monthly bulletin giving the time, station and an indication of the content of the broadcast. These are fine bulletin board displays and help to direct the 'out-of-school' listening as well as the 'in-school' listening.

Rural teachers should investigate the music lessons and programs which are theirs for a turn of the dial. It must be remembered that it is important for the class to have foundation instruction *before* the listening or viewing period, that everything must be in readiness for listening at the exact time of broadcast and that discussion after the listening period is essential for clarity and retention.

Many commercial recordings have been designed especially for classroom use. Fine recordings of rote songs can be used where the teacher feels inadequate in her own singing ability. Accompaniments have been recorded so that rural children may sing with an artistic accompaniment. Folk dances and folk songs; music for dancing, marching, games and rhythms; standard selections for listening and musical understanding are all procurable.

Some of the music text books in series have recordings made of illustrative material from the various music reading books. This gives the additional advantage of permitting the child to watch the music while the recordings are being heard.

While each rural school may wish to have its own small library of recordings so that certain selections will always be available, most public libraries have lending facilities and some state schools allow their music records to circulate. The lending regulations of larger schools in the immediate vicinity should be investigated.

Record catalogs contain not only listings of selections but also instructive information, pictures, and suggestions for the use of specific selections. They may be secured from the following major companies.

Columbia Recording Corporation, 1473 Barnum Ave., Bridgeport, Conn.
Decca Records, Inc., 50 W. 57th St., New York, N. Y.
General Records, Inc., 10 W. 4th St., New York, N. Y.
Musicraft Records, Inc., 10 W. 4th St., New York, N. Y.
R.C.A. Victory Company, Camden, N. J.

County Institutes and Workshops. Many counties have annual institutes which are held just preceding the opening of school or early in the school term. It is strongly recommended that at least one lecture on music should be included on every county institute program. Demonstration lessons showing how various phases of music can be taught will be found of great value and many opportunities to participate in singing should be included. Special music workshops for rural teachers will yield large dividends.

Unless music is successfully taught to all rural school children, musical illiteracy will not disappear. Successfully taught in rural communities, music will open the vast store of musical literature and thereby enrich and uplift the lives of a large number of our school children, the citizens of tomorrow.

APPENDIX A.

STATEMENT OF BELIEF AND PURPOSE

Throughout the ages, man has found music to be essential in voicing his own innate sense of beauty. Music is not a thing apart from man; it is the spiritualized expression of his finest and best inner self.

There is no one wholly unresponsive to the elevating appeal of music. If only the right contacts and experiences are provided, every life can find in music some answer to its fundamental need for aesthetic and emotional outlet. Education fails of its cultural objectives unless it brings to every child the consciousness that his own spirit may find satisfying expression through the arts.

The responsibility of offering every child a rich and varied experience in music rests upon the music teacher. It becomes his duty to see that music contributes its significant part in leading mankind to a higher plane of existence.

The Music Educators Conference, in full acceptance of its responsibilities as the representative and champion of progressive thought and practice in music education, pledges its united efforts in behalf of a broad and constructive program which shall include:

(1) Provision in all the schools of our country, both urban and rural, for musical experience and training for every child, in accordance with his interests and capacities.

(2) Continued effort to improve music teaching and to provide adequate equipment.

(3) Carry-over of school music training into the musical, social, and home life of the community, as a vital part of its cultural, recreational, and liesure-time activities.

(4) Increased opportunities for adult education in music.

(5) Improvement of choir and congregational singing in churches and Sunday Schools; increased use of instrumental ensemble playing in connection with church activities.

(6) Encouragement and support of all worthwhile musical enterprises as desirable factors in making our country a better place in which to live.

From Resolutions adopted by the Music Educators National Conference at its Biennial Meeting held in Los Angeles in 1940. The original statement, of which this is a simplified version, was first published in the *Music Educators Journal*, then the *Music Supervisors Journal* for October 1930.

Quoted from the *Music Education Source Book*, edited by Hazel Nohavec Morgan, Music Educators National Conference, Chicago, Illinois. 1947, p. iv.

APPENDIX B.

**AN AGREEMENT BY THE
AMERICAN FEDERATION OF MUSICIANS
MUSIC EDUCATORS NATIONAL CONFERENCE
AMERICAN ASSOCIATION OF SCHOOL ADMINISTRATORS
COVERING PUBLIC PERFORMANCE BY SCHOOL MUSICIANS**

A Code of Ethics

The competition of school bands and orchestras in the past years has been a matter of grave concern and, at times, even hardship to the professional musicians.

Music educators and professional musicians alike are committed to the general acceptance of music as a desirable factor in the social and cultural growth of our country. The music educators contribute to this end by fostering the study of music among the children, and by developing an interest in better music among the masses. The professional musicians strive to improve musical taste by providing increasingly artistic performances of worthwhile musical works.

This unanimity of purpose is further exemplified by the fact that a great many professional musicians are music educators, and a great many music educators are, or have been, actively engaged in the field of professional performance.

The members of high school symphonic orchestras and bands look to the professional organizations for example and inspiration; they become active patrons of music in later life. They are not content to listen to a twelve-piece ensemble when an orchestra of symphonic proportions is necessary to give adequate performance. These former music students, through their influence on sponsors, employers and program makers in demanding adequate musical performances, have a beneficial effect upon the prestige and economic status of the professional musicians.

Since it is in the interest of the music educator to attract public attention to his attainments for the purpose of enhancing his prestige and subsequently his income, and since it is in the interest of the professional musician to create more opportunities for employment at increased remuneration, it is only natural that upon certain occasions some incidents might occur in which the interests of the members of one or the other group might be infringed upon, either from lack of forethought or lack of ethical standards among individuals.

In order to establish a clear understanding as to the limitations of the fields of professional music and music education in the United States, the following statement of policy, adopted by the Music Educators National Conference and the American Federation of Musicians, and approved by the American Association of School Administrators, is recommended to those serving in their respective fields:

I. Music Education

The field of music education, including the teaching of music and such demonstrations of music education as do not directly conflict with the interests of the professional musician, is the province of the music educator. It is the primary purpose of all the parties signatory hereto that the professional musician shall have the fullest protection in his efforts to earn his living from the playing and rendition of music; to that end it is recognized and accepted that all music to be performed under the "Code of Ethics" herein set forth is and shall be performed in connection with non-profit, non-commercial and non-competitive enterprises. Under the heading of "Music Education" should be included the following:

(1) *School Functions* initiated by the schools as a part of a school program, whether in a school building or other building.

(2) *Community Functions* organized in the interest of the schools strictly for educational purposes, such as those that might be originated by the Parent-Teacher Association.

(3) *School Exhibits* prepared as a part of the school district's courtesies for educational organizations or educational conventions being entertained in the district.

(4) *Educational Broadcasts* which have the purpose of demonstrating or illustrating pupils' achievements in music study, or which represent the culmination of a period of study and rehearsal. Included in this category are local, state, regional and national school music festivals and competitions held under the auspices of schools, colleges, and/or educational organizations on a non-profit basis and broadcast to acquaint the public with the results of music instruction in the schools.

(5) *Civic Occasions* of local, state or national patriotic interest, of sufficient breadth to enlist the sympathies and cooperation of all persons, such as those held by the G.A.R., American Legion, and

Veterans of Foreign Wars in connection with their Memorial Day services in the cemeteries. It is understood that affairs of this kind may be participated in only when such participation does not in the least usurp the rights and privileges of local professional musicians.

(6) *Benefit Performances* for local charities, such as the Welfare Federations, Red Cross, hospitals, etc., and where local professional musicians would likewise donate their services.

(7) *Educational or Civic Services* that might beforehand be mutually agreed upon by the school authorities and official representatives of the local professional musicians.

(8) *Audition Recordings* for study purposes made in the classroom or in connection with contest or festival performances by students, such recordings to be limited to exclusive use by the students and their teachers, and not offered for general sale or other public distribution. This definition pertains only to the purpose and utilization of audition recordings and not to matters concerned with copyright regulations. Compliance with copyright requirements applying to recording of compositions not in the public domain is the responsibility of the school, college or educational organization under whose auspices the recording is made.

II. Entertainment

The field of entertainment is the province of the professional musician. Under this heading are the following:

(1) *Civic parades, ceremonies, expositions, community concerts, and community-center activities* (See I, Paragraph 2 for further definition); *regattas, non-scholastic contests, festivals, athletic games, activities or celebrations, and the like; national, state and county fairs* (See I, Paragraph 5 for further definition).

(2) *Functions for the furtherance, directly or indirectly, of any public or private enterprise; functions by chambers of commerce, boards of trade, and commercial clubs or associations.*

(3) *Any occasion that is partisan or sectarian in character or purpose.*

(4) *Functions of clubs, societies, civic or fraternal oragnizations.* Statements that funds are not available for the employment of professional musicians, or that if the talents of amateur musical organizations cannot be had, other musicians cannot or will not be employed, or that the amateur musicians are to play without remuneration of any kind, are all immaterial.

This Code shall remain in force for one year from September 22, 1947. At the end of one year the parties may come together for the purpose of making such revisions in this Code as they may deem necessary and as shall be mutually agreed upon.

JAMES C. PETRILLO
For American Federation of Musicians
LUTHER A. RICHMAN
For Music Educators National Conference
HEROLD C. HUNT
For American Association of School Administrators

Dated at Chicago, September 22, 1947.

APPENDIX C.

SAMPLE FORM FOR APPLIED MUSIC STUDY
TAKEN PRIVATELY OUTSIDE OF SCHOOL HOURS

....High School
OUTSIDE MUSIC COURSE APPLICATION FORM
We, the undersigned, hereby request that...
(Pupil's Name)
be admitted for credit to the music course herein named, subject to the regulations of the Board of Education governing the crediting of such courses, of which regulations this form is a part. These regulations we have read and hereby accept:
Voice or instrument...Grade of work..............................Term beginning
....Number of years of previous study without high school credit
....Number of years of previous study with high school credit

A year of thirty-six lessons of at least thirty minutes each ordinarily completes the work of a grade in music. Pupils are classified according to their accomplishment and will be marked for credit on the grade of work in which they are classified. Proper advance in grade each year is required for further credit.

Signed ....
Pupil
Signed ....
Parent
Signed ....
Teacher
Dated ....Record No.................

REPORT ON PRACTICE
Outside Music

....
(Name of School)
I hereby certify that..has spent the hours
enumerated below in practice in connection with..lessons
Week ending .... hours
Week ending .... hours
Week ending .... hours
Week ending .... hours
Total for the school period ending...hours

....
(Parent or guardian)
TEACHER'S REPORT ON INSTRUCTION AND PROGRESS
Outside Music

....
(Name of School)
Name ....Course in..
For the period from...........................to ....
Number of lessons...........................Length of each lesson............................
Techniques (Scales, etc.)............................
Studies ....
(Composer's name and opus number)
Pieces ....
(Title and composer)
Rating ....
....
Teacher

APPENDIX D.

PUBLISHER'S SUGGESTIONS FOR ORDERING MUSIC

Experience has shown that failure to comply with certain definite items unnecessarily delays music orders. It is advantageous to adhere to the following suggestions.

1. Be sure order is signed properly.
2. Legibility of hand-writing is absolutely necessary, both for details and for signatures.
3. Be sure that credit arrangements have been made, and proper billing instructions given.
4. Complete information should be given.
    a. Type of material—piano, band, octavo, etc.
    b. Voice arrangement—male, female, mixed, number of parts, etc.
    c. Edition—publisher (if possible).
    d. Arranger or composer.
    e. Type of instrumentation—exact parts, number of parts.
    f. If vocal solo, what voice? High, medium, low.
    g. Octavo music should include title as well as number.
    h. On approval, or 'Regular sale'.
5. Be sure information is correct.
    a. Conflict between arrangement desired and octavo number. Every vocal arrangement has a *different* octavo number.
    b. Conflict between arranger and voice arrangement. The arranger of the 2-part number, for example, did not always arrange the 3-part number of the same title.
    c. Be careful not to request arrangements not published.

APPENDIX E.

GENERAL TECHNICAL INFORMATION

Musicianship begins with basic technical information. The following provides a review of the theoretical material generally included in school music teaching and will be helpful for those students whose previous music training did not include this information. It should serve as a convenient reference for students and teachers.

Musical Terminology*

A cappella. Without accompaniment, generally referring to sacred choral music.

Accelerando. Gradually increasing the velocity.

Accent. Special stress or emphasis.

Accidentals. Occasional sharps, flats, or naturals, placed before notes in the course of a selection.

Adagio. Slow, quicker than largo but slower than andante.

Ad libitum. Freedom of interpretation, optional.

Affetto. Tenderly, with feeling.

Agilita. Lightly, airily.

Agitato. Hurried, agitated.

Al fine. To the end.

Allagrando. Growing broader, louder, and slower.

Allegretto. Light and cheery, not as quick as allegro.

Allegro. Quick, lively, vivacious.

Alto. The voice part between soprano and tenor, the voice which sings the alto part—either women or boys.

Andante. Moving, going, gracefully flowing.

Andantino. A little slower than andante.

Animato. With animation.

Appassionato. Passionately.

Appoggiatura. Grace note, embellishment.

Arioso. Melodious, graceful.

Arpeggio. The notes of a chord played quickly one after the other.

Art Song. A composed song as distinguished from a folk song, especially written by a master.

Assai. Very, or very much.

A tempo. In time, original speed.

Attack. Method of beginning a phrase.

A voix forte. With a loud voice.

Bar. A line drawn perpendicularly across the staff. The purpose of the bar is to divide the staff into measures.

Baritone. A voice or voice part between bass and tenor.

Bass. Lowest man's voice. Lowest part in vocal harmony.

Bel canto. Tender, pure, sympathetic.

Brilliante. Bright, sparkling.

Cadence. The ending of a phrase or other section of a composition, the effect of complete or partial close similar to punctuation in language.

Cantabile. Singing style, full of expression.

Capriccio. Free and vivacious style.

Celeste. Sweet toned, heavenly.

Chamber Music. Music for a small group of performers.

Choir. A company of singers. A section of an orchestra or band.

Chord. The union of two or more sounds heard at the same time.

Chromatic. Proceeding by semitones.

*In words derived from the Italian, every vowel is sounded separately, and is pronounced: a-ah, e-ā, i-ē, o-ō, u-ōō.

179

Clef. A character used to determine the name and pitch of the notes on the staff to which it is prefixed.

Con agilita. With agility, neatly.

Con animo. With life, animation.

Con brio. With spirit, brilliantly.

Con grazia. With grace, elegance.

Con moto. With motion, not dragging.

Con spirito. With spirit, life, energy.

Contralto. The lowest female voice.

Coloratura. Decorative, ornamental music, or the voice equipped to perform it.

Crescendo (cres. or <). With increasing power.

Da ballo. In dancing style.

Da capo (D.C.). Return to the beginning.

Dal Segno (D.S.). Return to the sign (S), a mark directing a repetition from the sign.

Descant. An optional counter melody.

Descriptive Music. Music suggesting a definite picture or story.

Diatonic. Proceeding in the order of the degrees of the natural scale.

Di gala. Merrily, cheerfully.

Diminuendo (dim. or >). Gradually diminishing the intensity of the tone.

Dolce. Sweetly, softly, delicately.

Dolore. Sorrow, grief.

Dot. A mark, which when placed *after* a note or rest increases its duration by one-half. When the dot is placed *above* a note it signifies that the note is to be staccato.

Double bar. Two thick lines drawn perpendicularly through the staff to divide one strain or movement from another; also used at the end of a piece.

Duet. For two voices or instruments.

Elegante. Graceful, elegant.

Embellishment. Ornamental tones; trill, turn, appoggiatura, etc.

Embouchure. Adjustment of the lips in playing a wind instrument.

Encore. Again, repeat by request.

Enharmonic. Different notation for the same pitch as A-sharp and B-flat.

Ensemble. Combination of performers.

Expressione. With expression, feeling.

Fermata. Hold (⌒). Placed over a note or rest indicating that the time value is to be prolonged.

Finale. The final part, conclusion.

Fine. The end, the termination.

Forte (f). Loud.

Forte mezzo (mf). Medium loud.

Fortissimo (ff). Very loud.

Fugue. An orderly contrapuntal treatment of a theme for three or more parts.

Gaudioso. Merrily, joyfully.

Giocoso. Jovially.

Grace note. A very short ornamental tone written as a small note with a dash through the flag.

Grandioso. Grand, noble.

Grazia. Grace, elegance.

Gusto. Taste, expression.

Interval. The difference in pitch between two tones.

Instrumentation. The art of arranging music for combinations of instruments.

Intonation. Exactness in pitch.

Largo. Slow and solemn movement.

Legato. Graceful and smooth; opposite of staccato.

Ma non troppo. But not too much.

Marcato. Accented, well marked.

Maestoso. Majestic, stately, dignified.

Marcia. As a march.

Measure. The space between two bars on the staff.

Mezzo. Medium.

Molto. Much.

Notes. Used to express duration of tone. (See illustration.)

Octave. An interval consisting of eleven half-steps or semitones.

Opus. Work. Many composers indicated the order of their works by opus number.

Phrase. The portion of a melody equivalent to a line of poetry.

Piano (p.). Soft.

Piano mezzo (mp). Medium soft.

Pianissimo (pp). Very soft.

Pizzicato. Meaning that the strings of the instrument are to be plucked and not bowed.

Poco. Little.

Poco a poco. Little by little.

Postlude. Instrumental conclusion of a song. A musical number closing a program or church service.

Prelude. Instrumental introduction to a song or instrumental suite. A musical number preceding a program, service, act of a play, etc.

Presto. Quick, rapidly.

Quartet. A group of four performers.

Quintet. A group of five performers.

Repeat bar. A character indicating that measures are to be played twice.

Rests. Characters indicating silence. (See illustration.)

Rhythm. The flow of musical tones as grouped by accents.

Ritardando (rit.) Gradually delaying the time.

Rondo. An instrumental composition in which the principal theme occurs several times with intervening contrasting themes. (Basic form, I - II - I - III - I).

Scherzo. A joke, hence a piece of music of playful or humorous character.

Serio. Grave, serious.

Sforzando. Emphasis, strength.

Semplice. Simply.

Sempre. Always.

Septet. A group of seven performers.

Sextet. A group of six performers.

Slur. A curved line drawn over or under two or more notes of different pitch indicating that they are to be executed legato.

Solo. To be presented by a single individual or instrument.

Soprano. The highest female voice or unchanged voice of a boy.

Sostenuto. Sustained.

Staccato. Detached, separated from each other.

Symphony. A sonata for orchestra.

Syncopation. A displacement of accent, either strong beats coming where weak ones are expected, or accents occurring off the beat.

Tenor. The highest adult male voice.

Tenuto. Sustained.

Tetrachord. A diatonic tone series within the interval of a fourth. Diatonic scales consist of two tetrachords, lower and upper, with similarities and differences which determine the character of the scale.

Theme. A brief melodic idea out of which a musical work or section of a composition is developed.

Tie. A curved line drawn over or under two or more notes of the same pitch indicating duration for the total value of the notes so connected.

Treble. Soprano.

Triad. A chord of three tones; root, third and fifth.

Trio. A group of three performers. The third section of a march or minuet.

Tranquillamente. Quietly, calmly, tranquilly.

Vivace. Lively, vivaciously.

Note and Rest Values

Time duration is indicated by various kinds of *notes* and *rests*. The chief ones encountered are the whole, half, quarter, eighths and sixteenth notes and rests. The comparative values are as follows.

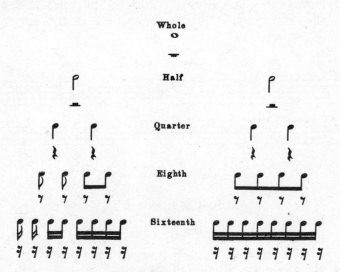

Intervals

The pitch relationship or distance between two tones is called an *interval*. It is called an interval whether the two tones are sounded simultaneously or successively. Theory and harmony classes often use specific names for intervals which are determined by the actual number of intervening steps and half-steps, (Major, minor, aug-

181

mented, diminished, perfect). *Numerical names* for intervals are determined by the relationship of the two tones upon the staff, for example:

The numerical name of any interval may be found by beginning with the degree of the staff on which the lower note is located and count the lines and spaces to the upper note, including both notes;

for example:  is an interval of a fourth.

The Great Staff

The *great staff* is composed of two five line staves commonly called the treble (upper) and bass (lower) plus a center line making a total of eleven lines. The letter names of the lines and spaces depend upon the clef which indicates whether it is the upper or lower portion of the great staff.

Key Signatures

The key in which a selection is indicated at the beginning of each staff, both treble and bass. The following rules apply to the proper location of the sharps and flats on the staff, and how to determine the major or minor key in which the composition is written.

(1) To *locate* the *sharps* on the staff, *treble clef*, always place the first sharp on the fifth line. Count down four, using the lines and spaces from the first sharp to locate the second sharp. Count up five from the second sharp to locate the third sharp, then continue counting down four and up five to locate the remaining sharps. Whenever the sharp falls outside of the staff or the first space above,

it is dropped down to the corresponding letter within the staff. Care must always be taken to begin counting with the sharp already located. For example:

To *locate* the *sharps* on the staff, *bass clef,* place the first sharp on the fourth line and proceed counting down four and up five to locate the subsequent sharps. For example:

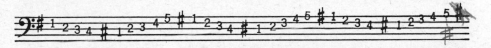

(2) To *locate* the *flats* on the staff, *treble clef,* always place the first flat on the third line. Count up four, using the lines and spaces, from the first flat to locate the second flat. Count down five from the second flat to locate the third flat, then continue counting up four and down five to locate the subsequent flats. Care must be taken to always begin counting with the flat already located. For example:

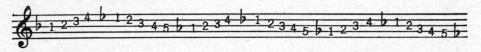

To *locate* the *flats* on the staff, *bass clef,* place the first flat on the second line and proceed counting up four and down five to locate the subsequent flats. For example:

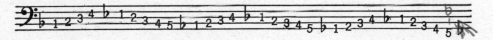

(3) If the *signature* has *sharps,* the last sharp to the right is called 'ti'. 'Do' is located the next place above 'ti'. Wherever 'do' is located is the major key letter name.

(4) If the signature has flats, the last flat to the right is called 'fa'. Count down four for the location of 'do'. Wherever 'do' is located is the major key letter name.

(5) If there are no sharps nor flats in the signature, the key of C major is indicated.

(6) The *minor key letter* name is taken from the location of the syllable 'la'. Use the rules above for the location of 'do' and count for the location of 'la'.

Care must be taken in naming any key letter to check back through the signature to see if the letter named has been affected by a sharp or flat. If the place where the key letter falls has been affected, then the word 'sharp' or 'flat' must be added to the key letter name.

Time Signatures

Two numbers, one above the other, will be found at the beginning of the first staff of the composition. The upper number indicates how many counts or beats are to be found in each measure. The lower number indicates what kind of a note is to receive one count or beat. For example, indicates that there are three beats in each measure and that a quarter note should receive one beat, or indicates that there are six beats to each measure and that an eighth note should receive one beat or count.

184

Index